WHAT? ME? A RACIST?

HEY, THEO, WHAT'S UP, DID YOU FALL OUT OF BED OR SOMETHING?
YEAH, I DID, MUM. AS MARTIN LUTHER KING SAID, 'I HAD A DREAM'.
SPIKE LEE DO THE RIGHT THING
PORTISHEAD
LIVE

The European Union is determined to combat discrimination on grounds of sex, race, ethnic origin, religion or belief, disability, age or sexual orientation. This humorously written and informative pamphlet has been designed for teachers to use when addressing the subject of racism with young people.

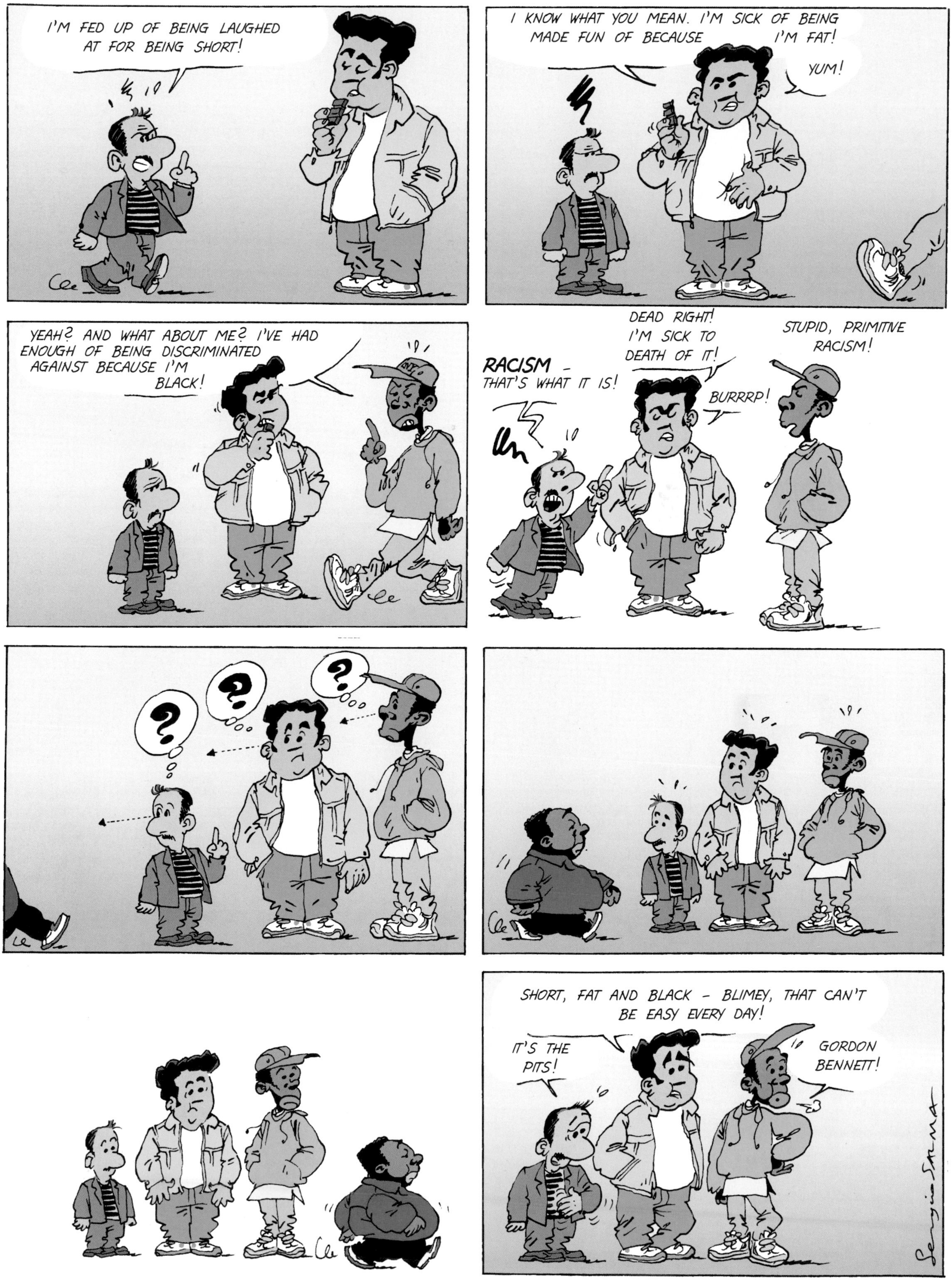
I'M FED UP OF BEING LAUGHED AT FOR BEING SHORT!
I KNOW WHAT YOU MEAN. I'M SICK OF BEING MADE FUN OF BECAUSE I'M FAT!
YUM!
YEAH? AND WHAT ABOUT ME? I'VE HAD ENOUGH OF BEING DISCRIMINATED AGAINST BECAUSE I'M BLACK!
RACISM - THAT'S WHAT IT IS!
DEAD RIGHT! I'M SICK TO DEATH OF IT!
BURRRP!
STUPID, PRIMITIVE RACISM!
SHORT, FAT AND BLACK - BLIMEY, THAT CAN'T BE EASY EVERY DAY!
IT'S THE PITS!
GORDON BENNETT!

FACE VALUE

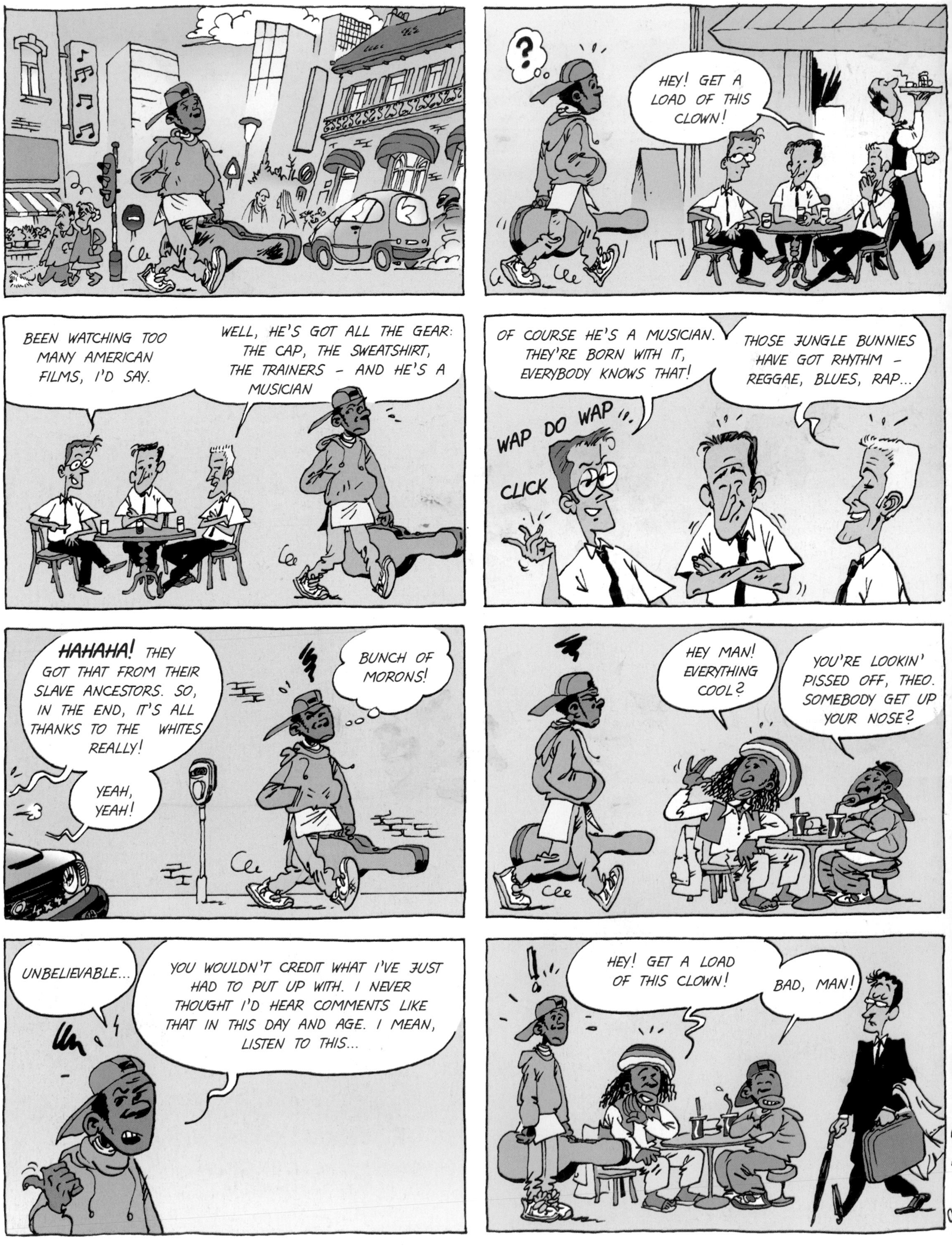
HEY! GET A LOAD OF THIS CLOWN!
BEEN WATCHING TOO MANY AMERICAN FILMS, I'D SAY.
WELL, HE'S GOT ALL THE GEAR: THE CAP, THE SWEATSHIRT, THE TRAINERS - AND HE'S A MUSICIAN
OF COURSE HE'S A MUSICIAN. THEY'RE BORN WITH IT, EVERYBODY KNOWS THAT!
THOSE JUNGLE BUNNIES HAVE GOT RHYTHM - REGGAE, BLUES, RAP...
WAP DO WAP
CLICK
HAHAHA! THEY GOT THAT FROM THEIR SLAVE ANCESTORS. SO, IN THE END, IT'S ALL THANKS TO THE WHITES REALLY!
YEAH, YEAH!
BUNCH OF MORONS!
HEY MAN! EVERYTHING COOL?
YOU'RE LOOKIN' PISSED OFF, THEO. SOMEBODY GET UP YOUR NOSE?
UNBELIEVABLE...
YOU WOULDN'T CREDIT WHAT I'VE JUST HAD TO PUT UP WITH. I NEVER THOUGHT I'D HEAR COMMENTS LIKE THAT IN THIS DAY AND AGE. I MEAN, LISTEN TO THIS...
HEY! GET A LOAD OF THIS CLOWN!
BAD, MAN!

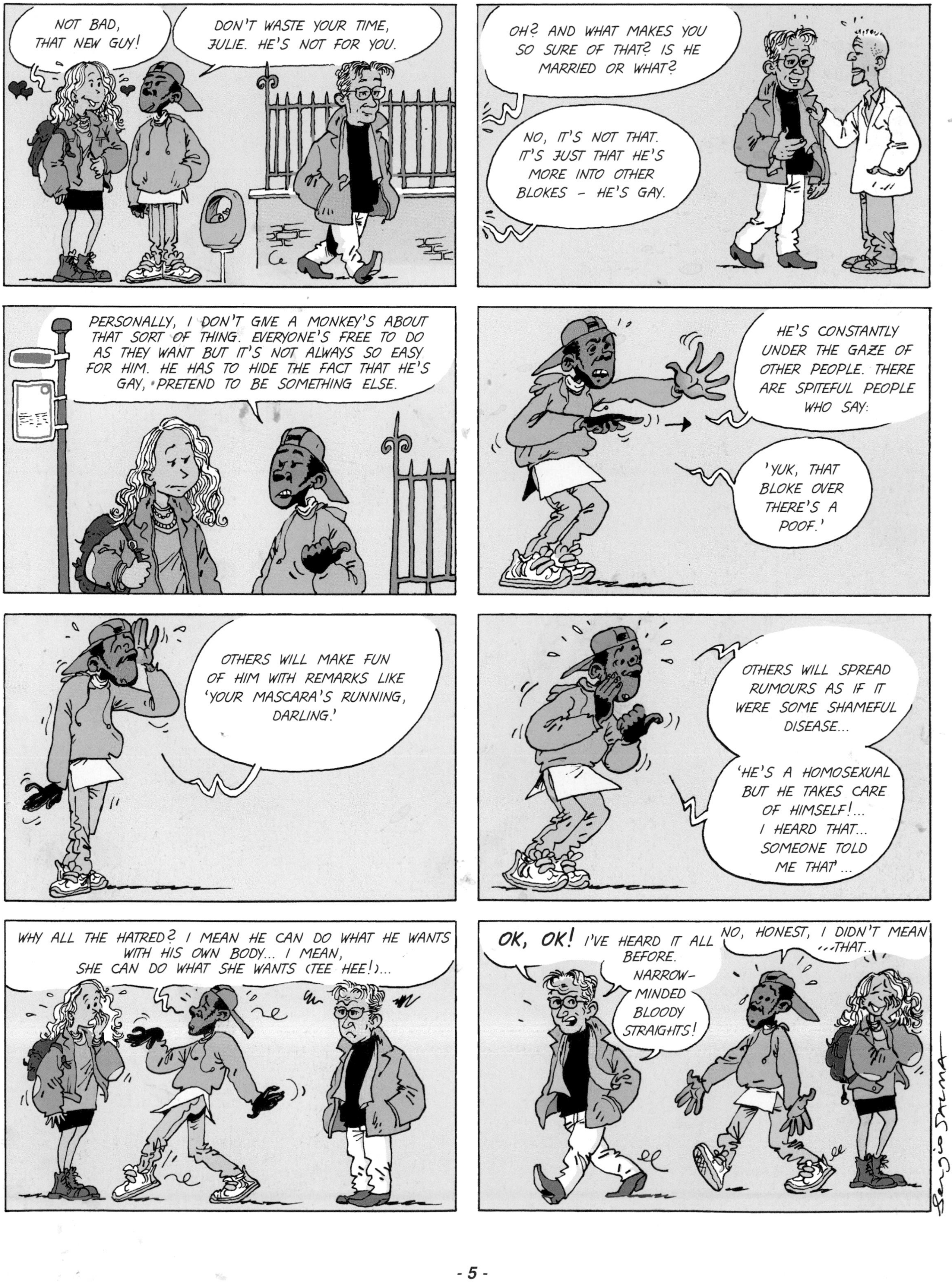
NOT BAD, THAT NEW GUY!
DON'T WASTE YOUR TIME, JULIE. HE'S NOT FOR YOU.
OH? AND WHAT MAKES YOU SO SURE OF THAT? IS HE MARRIED OR WHAT?
NO, IT'S NOT THAT. IT'S JUST THAT HE'S MORE INTO OTHER BLOKES – HE'S GAY.
PERSONALLY, I DON'T GIVE A MONKEY'S ABOUT THAT SORT OF THING. EVERYONE'S FREE TO DO AS THEY WANT BUT IT'S NOT ALWAYS SO EASY FOR HIM. HE HAS TO HIDE THE FACT THAT HE'S GAY, PRETEND TO BE SOMETHING ELSE.
HE'S CONSTANTLY UNDER THE GAZE OF OTHER PEOPLE. THERE ARE SPITEFUL PEOPLE WHO SAY:
'YUK, THAT BLOKE OVER THERE'S A POOF.'
OTHERS WILL MAKE FUN OF HIM WITH REMARKS LIKE 'YOUR MASCARA'S RUNNING, DARLING.'
OTHERS WILL SPREAD RUMOURS AS IF IT WERE SOME SHAMEFUL DISEASE...
'HE'S A HOMOSEXUAL BUT HE TAKES CARE OF HIMSELF!... I HEARD THAT... SOMEONE TOLD ME THAT'...
WHY ALL THE HATRED? I MEAN HE CAN DO WHAT HE WANTS WITH HIS OWN BODY... I MEAN, SHE CAN DO WHAT SHE WANTS (TEE HEE!)...
OK, OK! I'VE HEARD IT ALL BEFORE. NARROW-MINDED BLOODY STRAIGHTS!
NO, HONEST, I DIDN'T MEAN THAT...
Sergio Salma

CHAIN RACISM

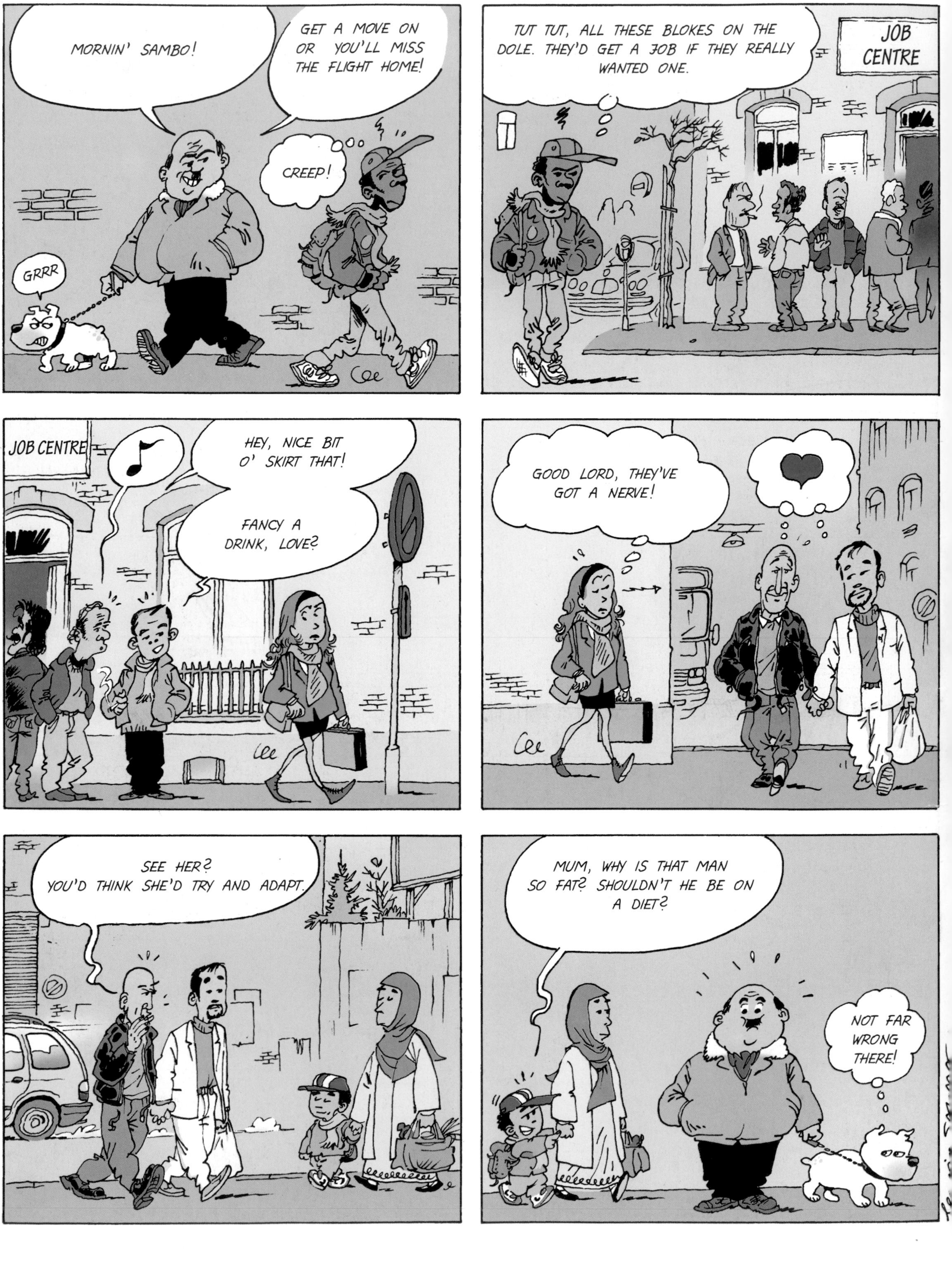
MORNIN' SAMBO!
GET A MOVE ON OR YOU'LL MISS THE FLIGHT HOME!
CREEP!
GRRR
TUT TUT, ALL THESE BLOKES ON THE DOLE. THEY'D GET A JOB IF THEY REALLY WANTED ONE.
JOB CENTRE
JOB CENTRE
HEY, NICE BIT O' SKIRT THAT!
FANCY A DRINK, LOVE?
GOOD LORD, THEY'VE GOT A NERVE!
SEE HER? YOU'D THINK SHE'D TRY AND ADAPT.
MUM, WHY IS THAT MAN SO FAT? SHOULDN'T HE BE ON A DIET?
NOT FAR WRONG THERE!

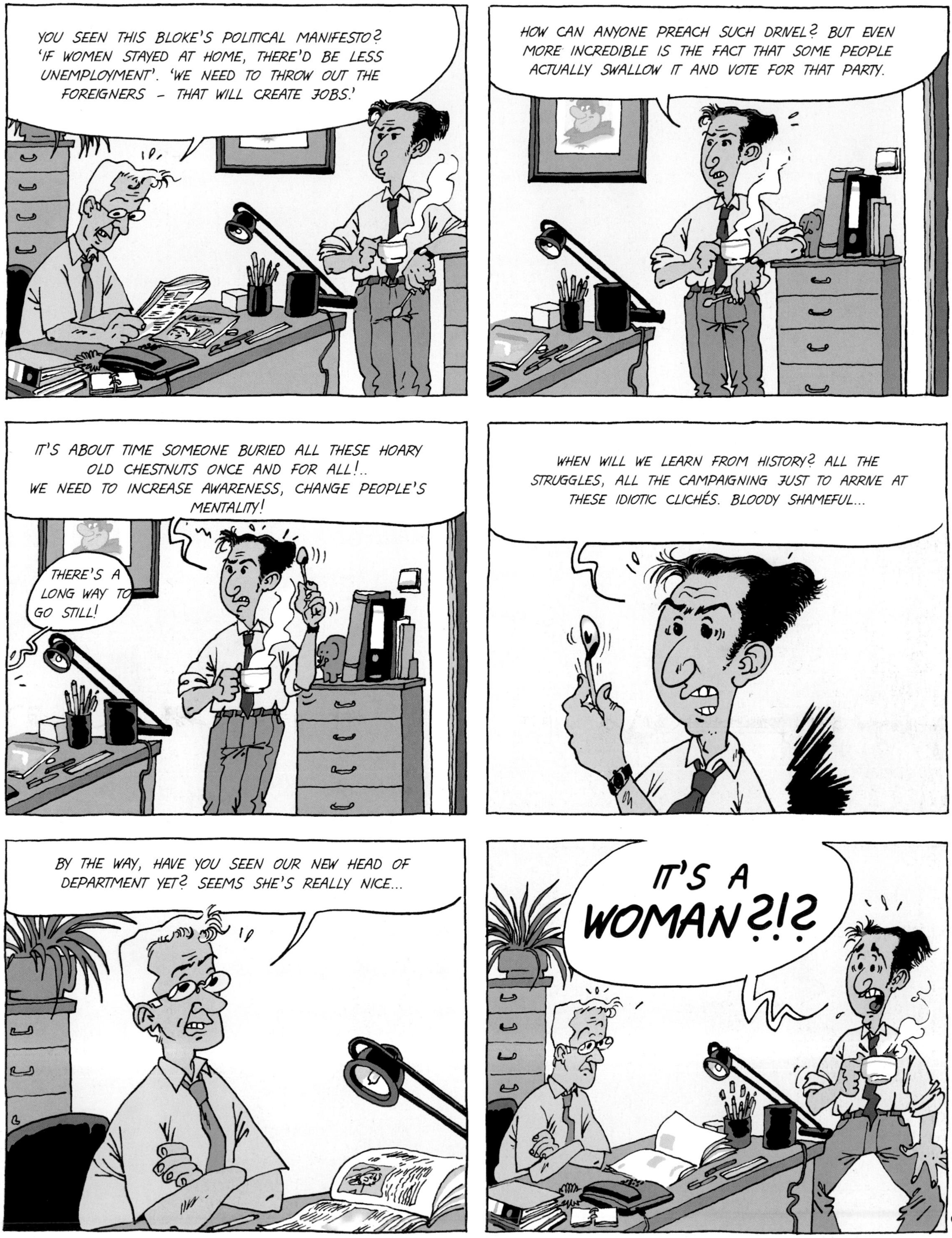
YOU SEEN THIS BLOKE'S POLITICAL MANIFESTO? 'IF WOMEN STAYED AT HOME, THERE'D BE LESS UNEMPLOYMENT'. 'WE NEED TO THROW OUT THE FOREIGNERS – THAT WILL CREATE JOBS.'
HOW CAN ANYONE PREACH SUCH DRIVEL? BUT EVEN MORE INCREDIBLE IS THE FACT THAT SOME PEOPLE ACTUALLY SWALLOW IT AND VOTE FOR THAT PARTY.
IT'S ABOUT TIME SOMEONE BURIED ALL THESE HOARY OLD CHESTNUTS ONCE AND FOR ALL!.. WE NEED TO INCREASE AWARENESS, CHANGE PEOPLE'S MENTALITY!
THERE'S A LONG WAY TO GO STILL!
WHEN WILL WE LEARN FROM HISTORY? ALL THE STRUGGLES, ALL THE CAMPAIGNING JUST TO ARRIVE AT THESE IDIOTIC CLICHÉS. BLOODY SHAMEFUL...
BY THE WAY, HAVE YOU SEEN OUR NEW HEAD OF DEPARTMENT YET? SEEMS SHE'S REALLY NICE...
IT'S A WOMAN?!?

WHITER THAN WHITE

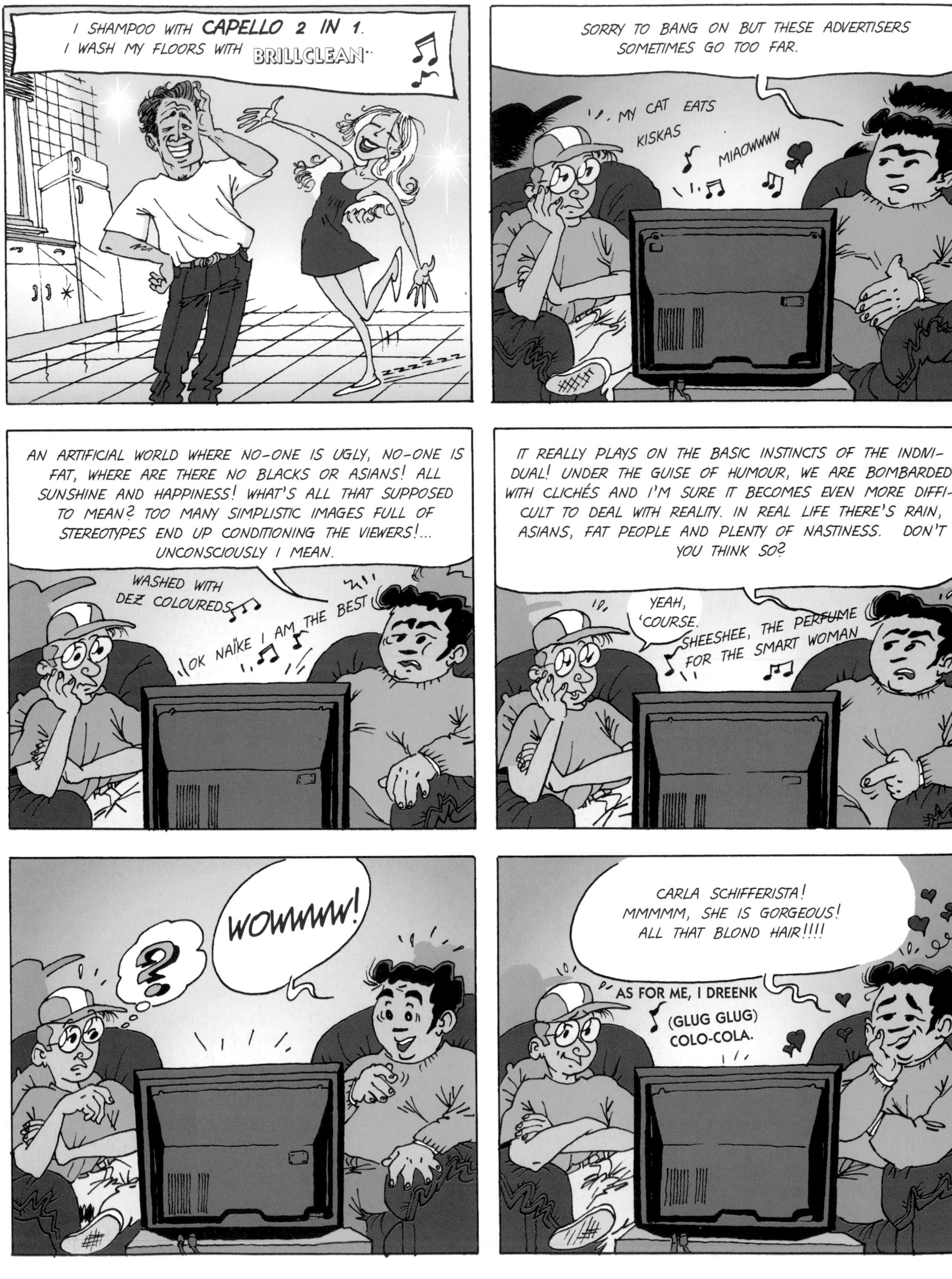

I SHAMPOO WITH CAPELLO 2 IN 1.
I WASH MY FLOORS WITH BRILLCLEAN
SORRY TO BANG ON BUT THESE ADVERTISERS SOMETIMES GO TOO FAR.
MY CAT EATS KISKAS
MIAOWWWW
AN ARTIFICIAL WORLD WHERE NO-ONE IS UGLY, NO-ONE IS FAT, WHERE ARE THERE NO BLACKS OR ASIANS! ALL SUNSHINE AND HAPPINESS! WHAT'S ALL THAT SUPPOSED TO MEAN? TOO MANY SIMPLISTIC IMAGES FULL OF STEREOTYPES END UP CONDITIONING THE VIEWERS!... UNCONSCIOUSLY I MEAN.
WASHED WITH DEZ COLOUREDS
OK NAÏKE I AM THE BEST
IT REALLY PLAYS ON THE BASIC INSTINCTS OF THE INDIVIDUAL! UNDER THE GUISE OF HUMOUR, WE ARE BOMBARDED WITH CLICHÉS AND I'M SURE IT BECOMES EVEN MORE DIFFICULT TO DEAL WITH REALITY. IN REAL LIFE THERE'S RAIN, ASIANS, FAT PEOPLE AND PLENTY OF NASTINESS. DON'T YOU THINK SO?
YEAH, 'COURSE.
SHEESHEE, THE PERFUME FOR THE SMART WOMAN
WOWWWW!
CARLA SCHIFFERISTA! MMMMM, SHE IS GORGEOUS! ALL THAT BLOND HAIR!!!!
AS FOR ME, I DREENK (GLUG GLUG) COLO-COLA.

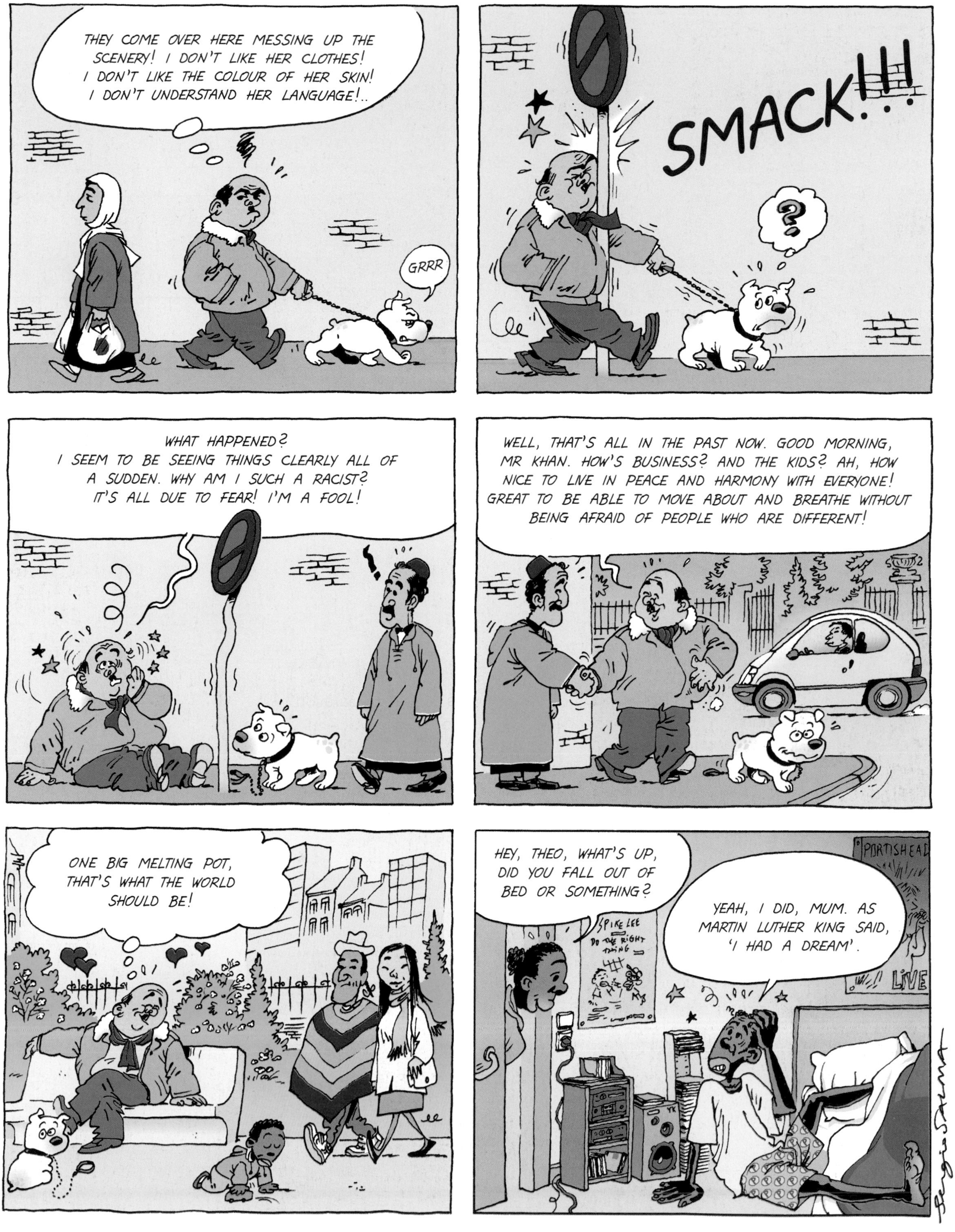
THEY COME OVER HERE MESSING UP THE SCENERY! I DON'T LIKE HER CLOTHES! I DON'T LIKE THE COLOUR OF HER SKIN! I DON'T UNDERSTAND HER LANGUAGE!..
GRRR
SMACK!!!
WHAT HAPPENED? I SEEM TO BE SEEING THINGS CLEARLY ALL OF A SUDDEN. WHY AM I SUCH A RACIST? IT'S ALL DUE TO FEAR! I'M A FOOL!
WELL, THAT'S ALL IN THE PAST NOW. GOOD MORNING, MR KHAN. HOW'S BUSINESS? AND THE KIDS? AH, HOW NICE TO LIVE IN PEACE AND HARMONY WITH EVERYONE! GREAT TO BE ABLE TO MOVE ABOUT AND BREATHE WITHOUT BEING AFRAID OF PEOPLE WHO ARE DIFFERENT!
ONE BIG MELTING POT, THAT'S WHAT THE WORLD SHOULD BE!
HEY, THEO, WHAT'S UP, DID YOU FALL OUT OF BED OR SOMETHING?
SPIKE LEE
DO THE RIGHT THING
PORTISHEAD
LIVE
YEAH, I DID, MUM. AS MARTIN LUTHER KING SAID, 'I HAD A DREAM'.

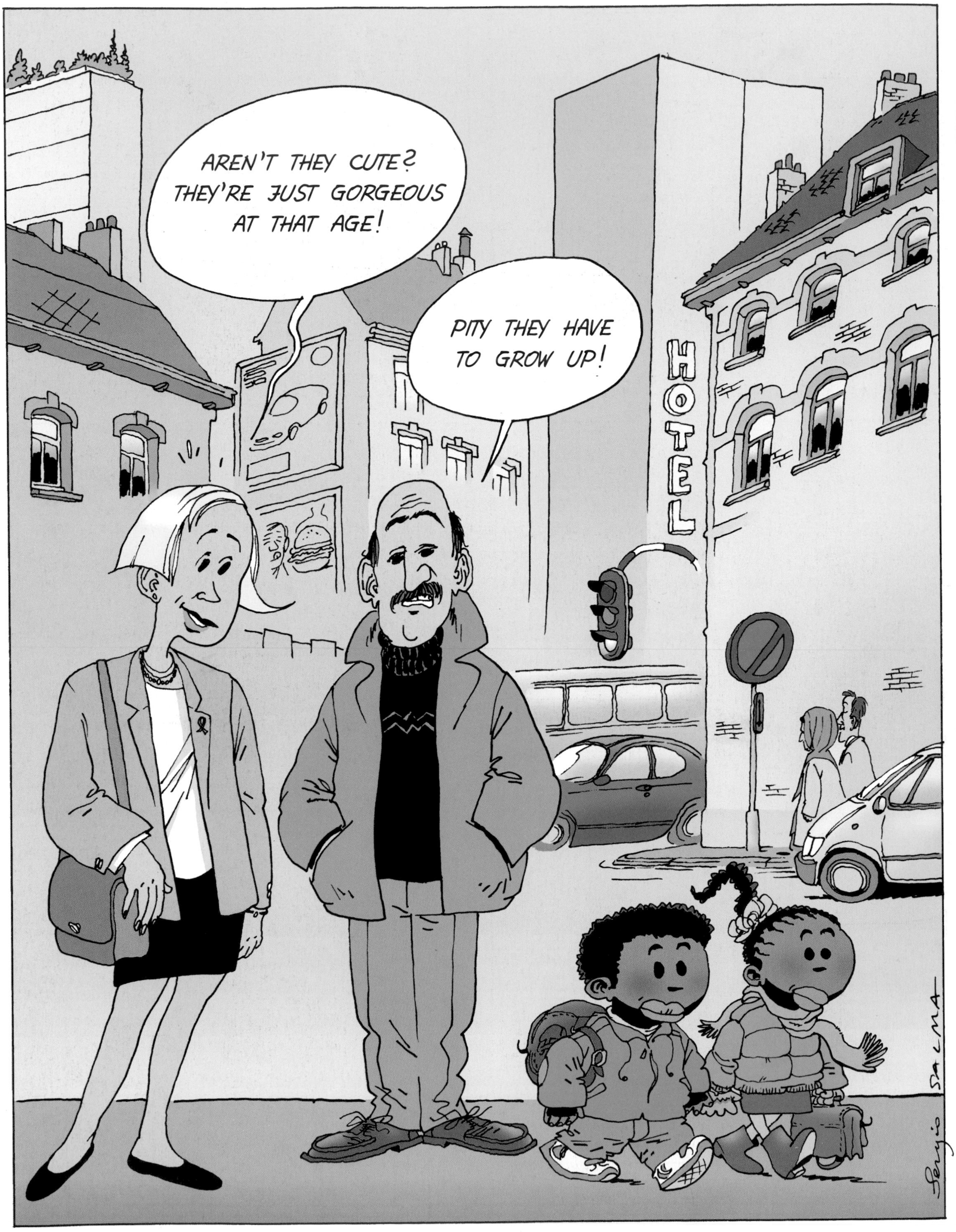
AREN'T THEY CUTE? THEY'RE JUST GORGEOUS AT THAT AGE!
PITY THEY HAVE TO GROW UP!
HOTEL
Sergio SALMA

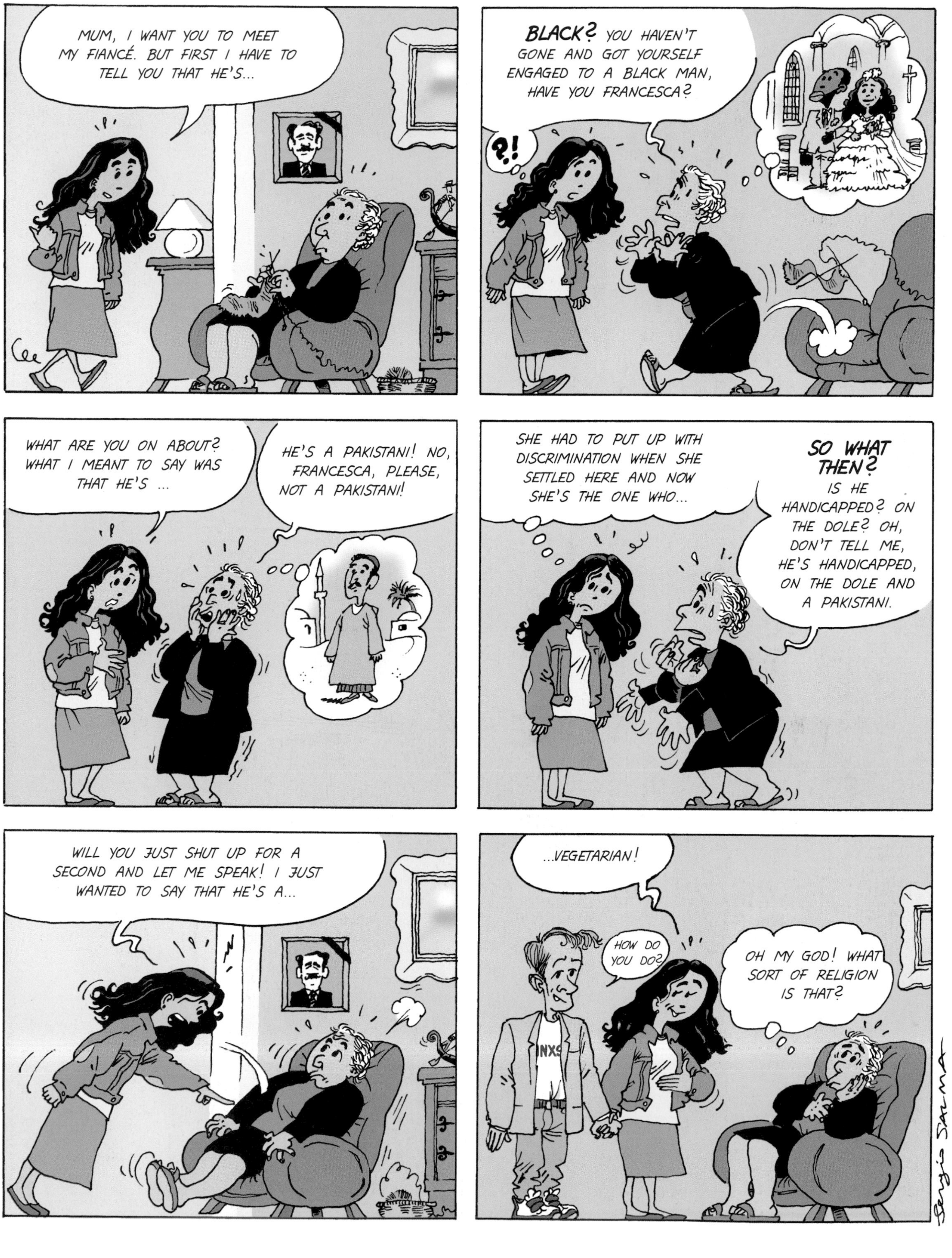
MUM, I WANT YOU TO MEET MY FIANCÉ. BUT FIRST I HAVE TO TELL YOU THAT HE'S...
BLACK? YOU HAVEN'T GONE AND GOT YOURSELF ENGAGED TO A BLACK MAN, HAVE YOU FRANCESCA?
?!
WHAT ARE YOU ON ABOUT? WHAT I MEANT TO SAY WAS THAT HE'S ...
HE'S A PAKISTANI! NO, FRANCESCA, PLEASE, NOT A PAKISTANI!
SHE HAD TO PUT UP WITH DISCRIMINATION WHEN SHE SETTLED HERE AND NOW SHE'S THE ONE WHO...
SO WHAT THEN? IS HE HANDICAPPED? ON THE DOLE? OH, DON'T TELL ME, HE'S HANDICAPPED, ON THE DOLE AND A PAKISTANI.
WILL YOU JUST SHUT UP FOR A SECOND AND LET ME SPEAK! I JUST WANTED TO SAY THAT HE'S A...
...VEGETARIAN!
HOW DO YOU DO?
INXS
OH MY GOD! WHAT SORT OF RELIGION IS THAT?
Sergio Salma

GETTING IN TRIM

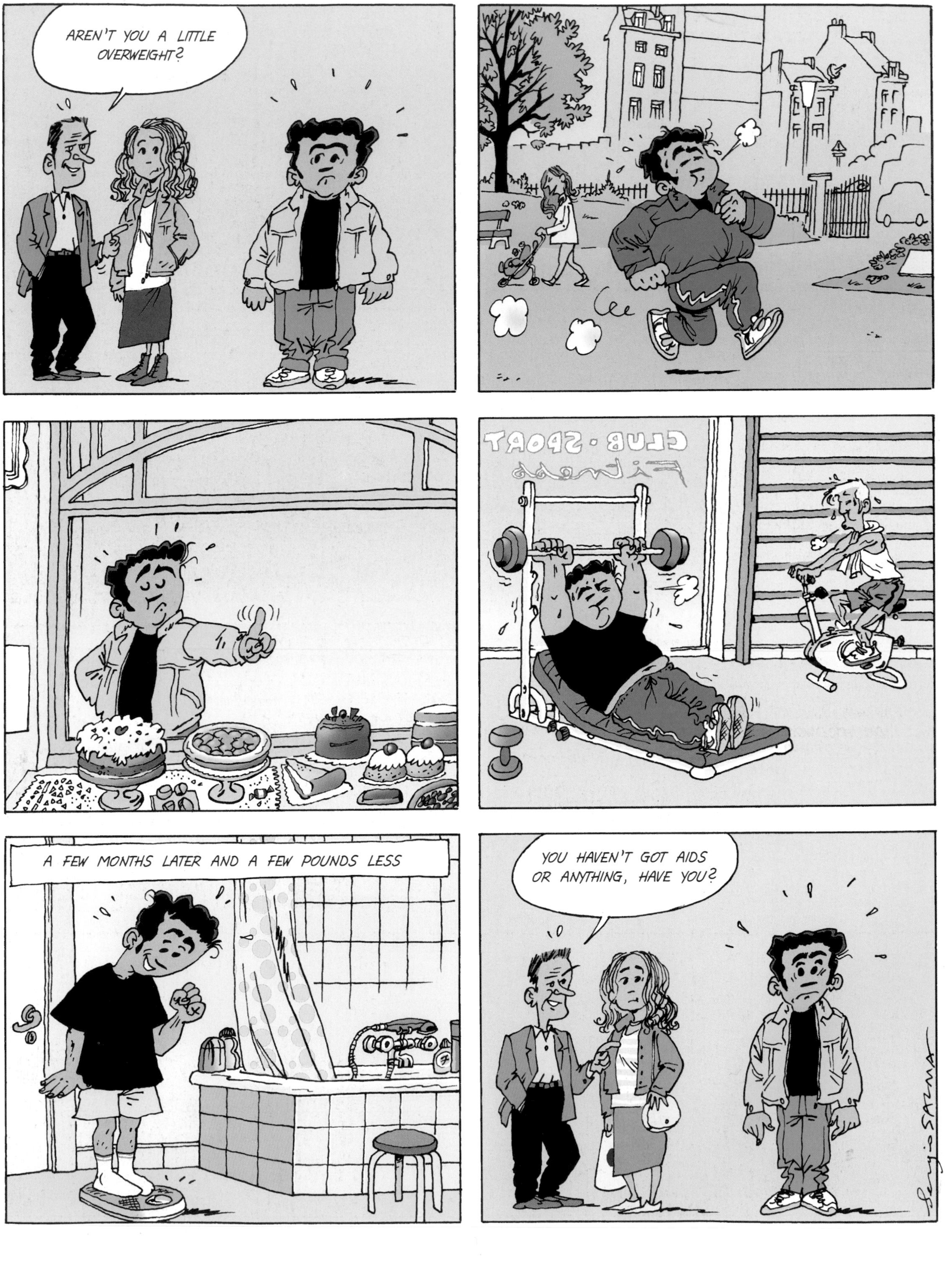
AREN'T YOU A LITTLE OVERWEIGHT?
A FEW MONTHS LATER AND A FEW POUNDS LESS
YOU HAVEN'T GOT AIDS OR ANYTHING, HAVE YOU?
Sergio SALMA

THIS IS MY COUSIN, TONY. DON'T BE SCARED. HE'S A BIT, WELL, DIFFERENT BUT HE'S OKAY.

HI, TONY. I'M THEO.

HI! I'M FRANCESCA.

HULLO!

HE LOOKS WORSE THAN I EXPECTED. BETTER JUST ACT NATURAL.

MUST TRY NOT TO LOOK NERVOUS.

I THOUGHT PERHAPS WE COULD GO TO THE CINEMA.

CINEMA? HE WANTS HIS HEAD READ! HIS COUSIN'LL NEVER KEEP UP!

NOT SURE TONY'LL LIKE IT.

YEAH, GOOD IDEA!

WHY NOT?

CINEMA.

HERE, LET'S SEE WHAT'S ON.

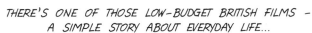

THERE'S ONE OF THOSE LOW-BUDGET BRITISH FILMS - A SIMPLE STORY ABOUT EVERYDAY LIFE...

OR WHAT ABOUT A BIG HOLLYWOOD ACTION FILM?

'DESTRUCTOR IV' FOR EXAMPLE

FREDDY MUST BE OFF HIS TROLLEY! WE DON'T WANT ANYTHING COMPLICATED OR HIS COUSIN'LL BE OUT OF HIS DEPTH.

SOMETHING WITH NO DIALOGUE SO TONY CAN FOLLOW IT.

ALL RIGHT, COME ON - WE'VE GOT TO DECIDE ON SOMETHING. WHY NOT AN OLD BLACK-AND-WHITE FILM. THERE'S ONE HERE SOMEWHERE WITH TONY CURTIS AND MARILYN MONROE. NOW WHAT WAS IT CALLED AGAIN?...

'SOME LIKE IT HOT', BILLY WILDER, 1953.

PREJUDICES

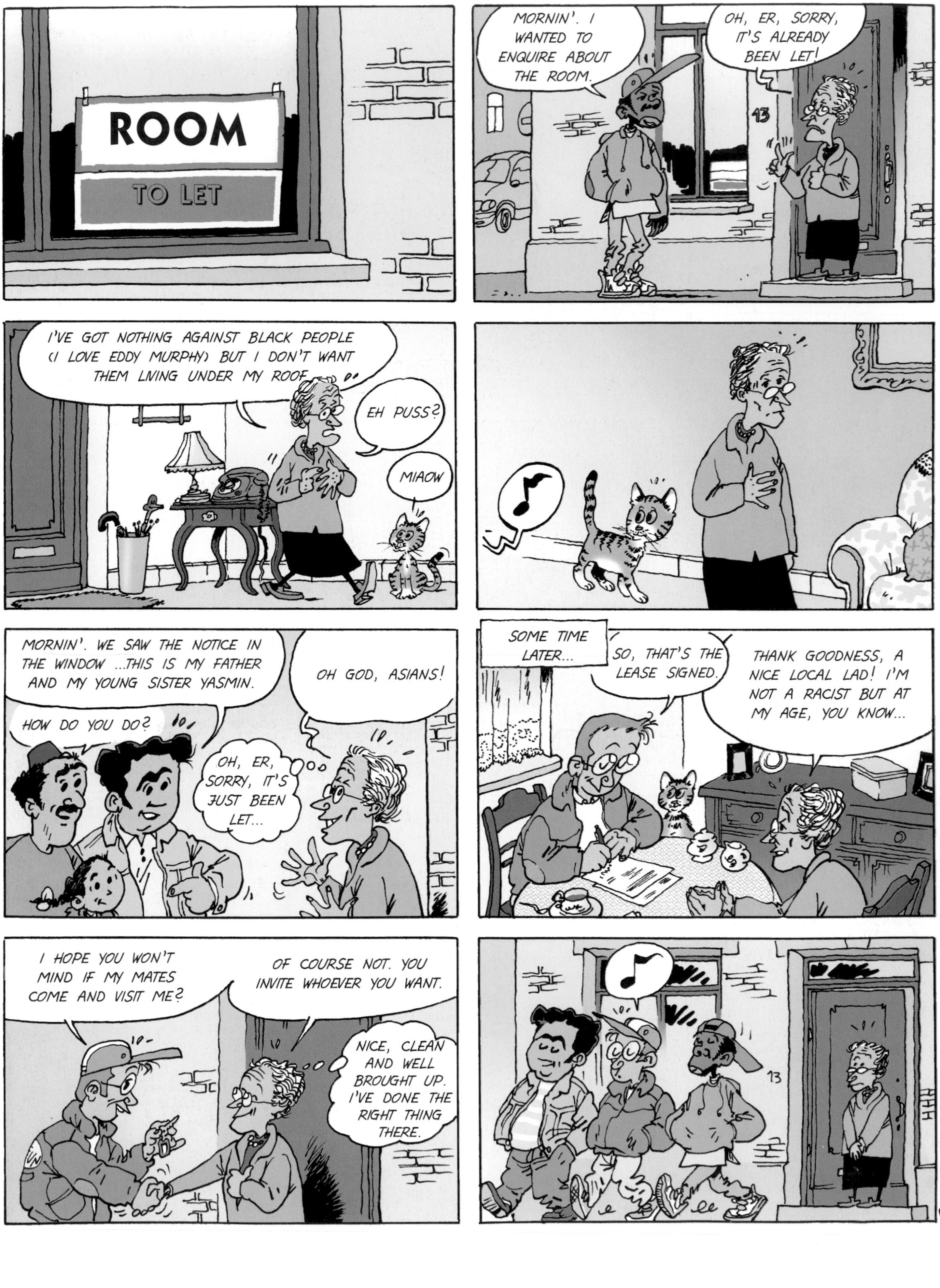
ROOM
TO LET
MORNIN'. I WANTED TO ENQUIRE ABOUT THE ROOM.
OH, ER, SORRY, IT'S ALREADY BEEN LET!
13
I'VE GOT NOTHING AGAINST BLACK PEOPLE (I LOVE EDDY MURPHY) BUT I DON'T WANT THEM LIVING UNDER MY ROOF
EH PUSS?
MIAOW
MORNIN'. WE SAW THE NOTICE IN THE WINDOW ...THIS IS MY FATHER AND MY YOUNG SISTER YASMIN.
HOW DO YOU DO?
OH GOD, ASIANS!
OH, ER, SORRY, IT'S JUST BEEN LET...
SOME TIME LATER...
SO, THAT'S THE LEASE SIGNED.
THANK GOODNESS, A NICE LOCAL LAD! I'M NOT A RACIST BUT AT MY AGE, YOU KNOW...
I HOPE YOU WON'T MIND IF MY MATES COME AND VISIT ME?
OF COURSE NOT. YOU INVITE WHOEVER YOU WANT.
NICE, CLEAN AND WELL BROUGHT UP. I'VE DONE THE RIGHT THING THERE.
13

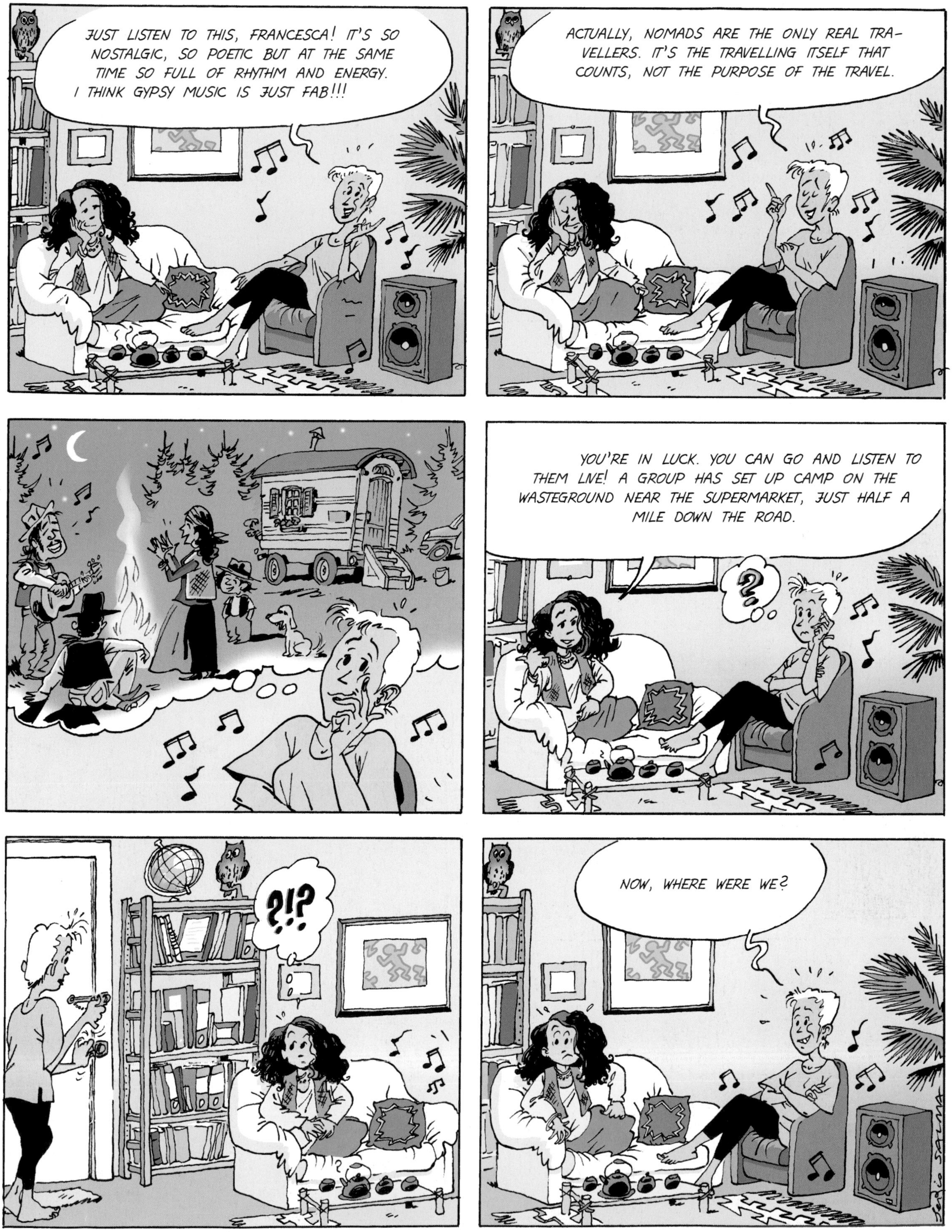
JUST LISTEN TO THIS, FRANCESCA! IT'S SO NOSTALGIC, SO POETIC BUT AT THE SAME TIME SO FULL OF RHYTHM AND ENERGY. I THINK GYPSY MUSIC IS JUST FAB!!!
ACTUALLY, NOMADS ARE THE ONLY REAL TRAVELLERS. IT'S THE TRAVELLING ITSELF THAT COUNTS, NOT THE PURPOSE OF THE TRAVEL.
YOU'RE IN LUCK. YOU CAN GO AND LISTEN TO THEM LIVE! A GROUP HAS SET UP CAMP ON THE WASTEGROUND NEAR THE SUPERMARKET, JUST HALF A MILE DOWN THE ROAD.
?
?!?
NOW, WHERE WERE WE?
SERGIO SALMA

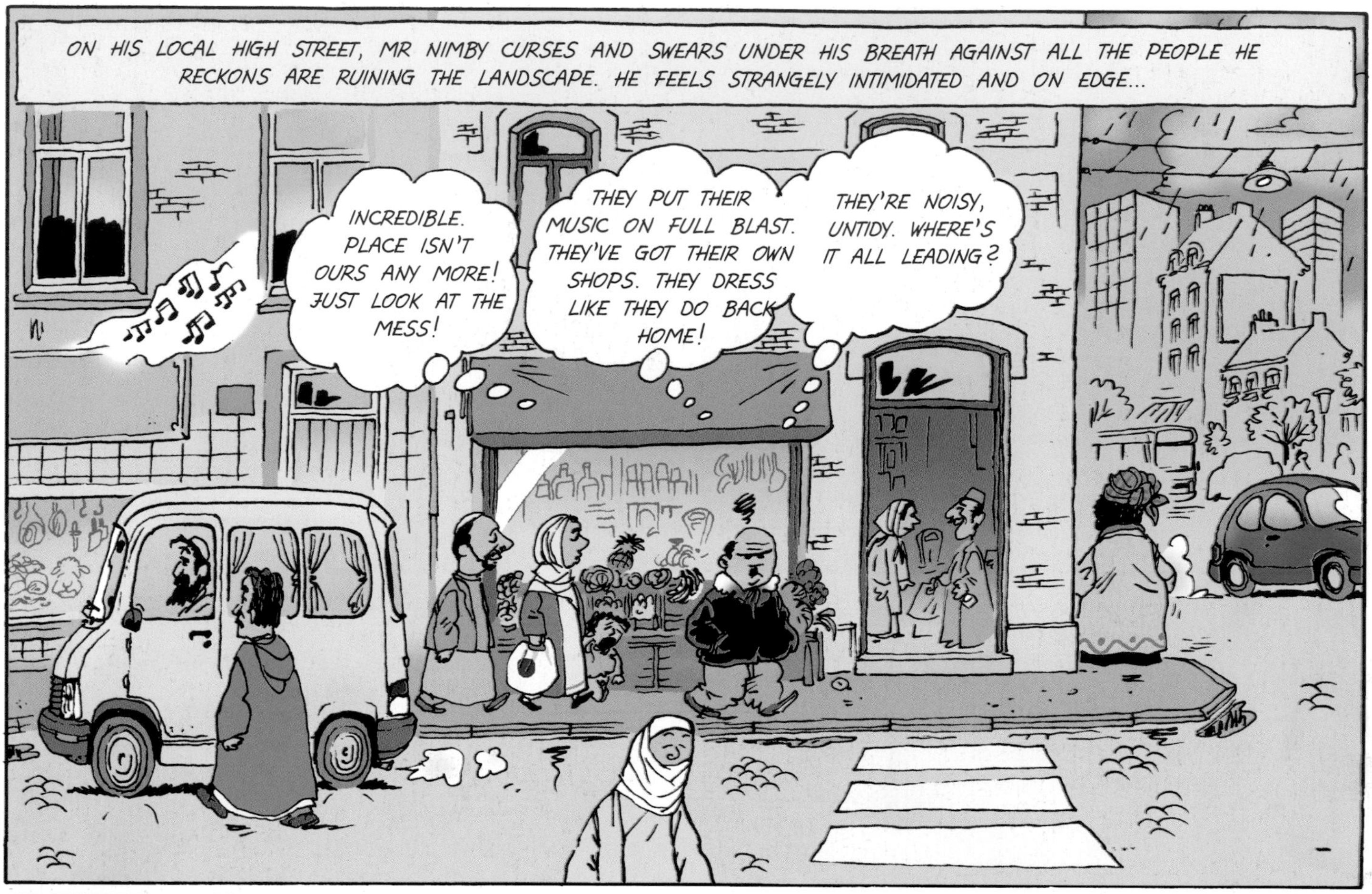
ON HIS LOCAL HIGH STREET, MR NIMBY CURSES AND SWEARS UNDER HIS BREATH AGAINST ALL THE PEOPLE HE RECKONS ARE RUINING THE LANDSCAPE. HE FEELS STRANGELY INTIMIDATED AND ON EDGE...
INCREDIBLE. PLACE ISN'T OURS ANY MORE! JUST LOOK AT THE MESS!
THEY PUT THEIR MUSIC ON FULL BLAST. THEY'VE GOT THEIR OWN SHOPS. THEY DRESS LIKE THEY DO BACK HOME!
THEY'RE NOISY, UNTIDY. WHERE'S IT ALL LEADING?

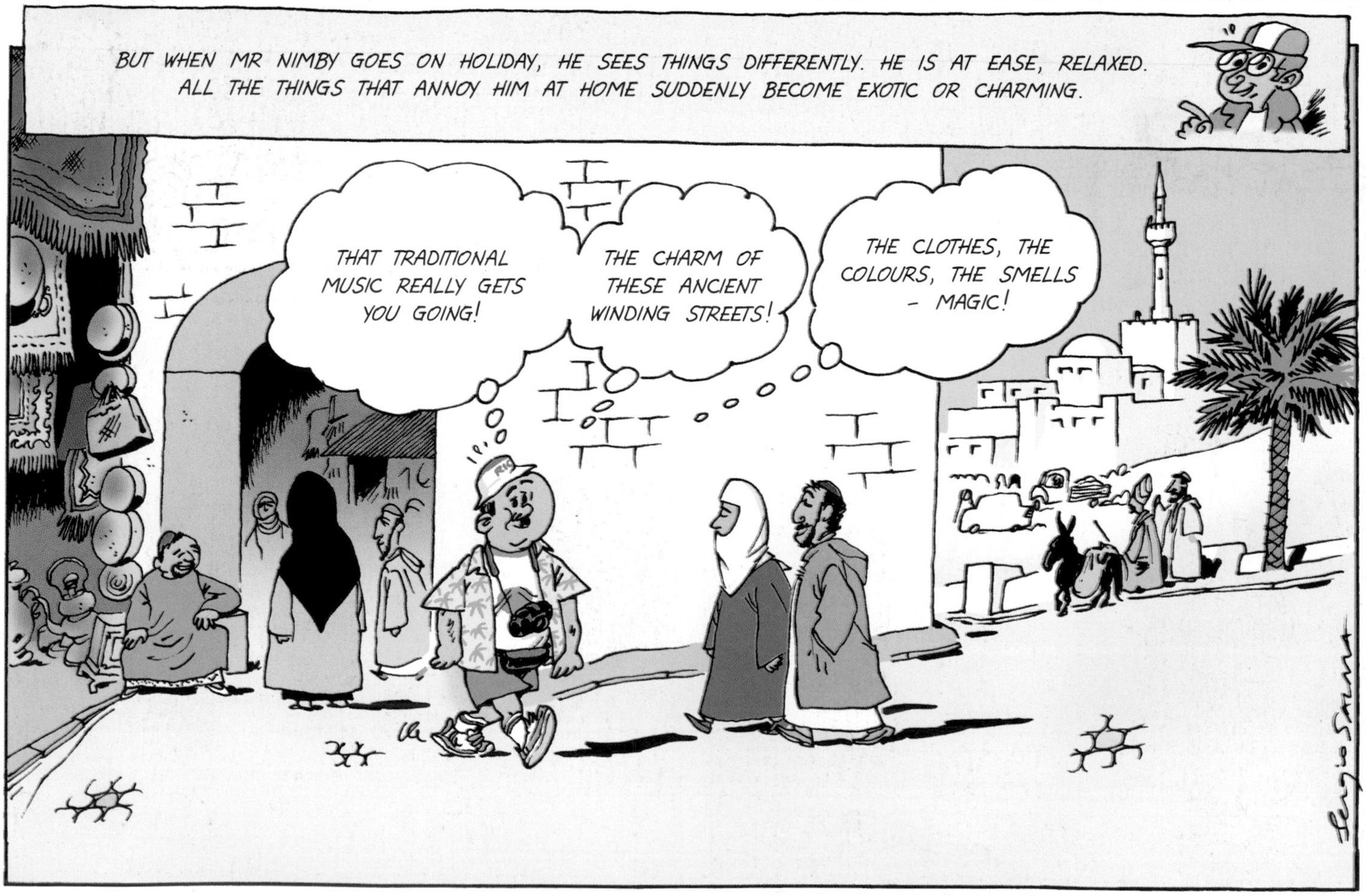
BUT WHEN MR NIMBY GOES ON HOLIDAY, HE SEES THINGS DIFFERENTLY. HE IS AT EASE, RELAXED. ALL THE THINGS THAT ANNOY HIM AT HOME SUDDENLY BECOME EXOTIC OR CHARMING.
THAT TRADITIONAL MUSIC REALLY GETS YOU GOING!
THE CHARM OF THESE ANCIENT WINDING STREETS!
THE CLOTHES, THE COLOURS, THE SMELLS - MAGIC!

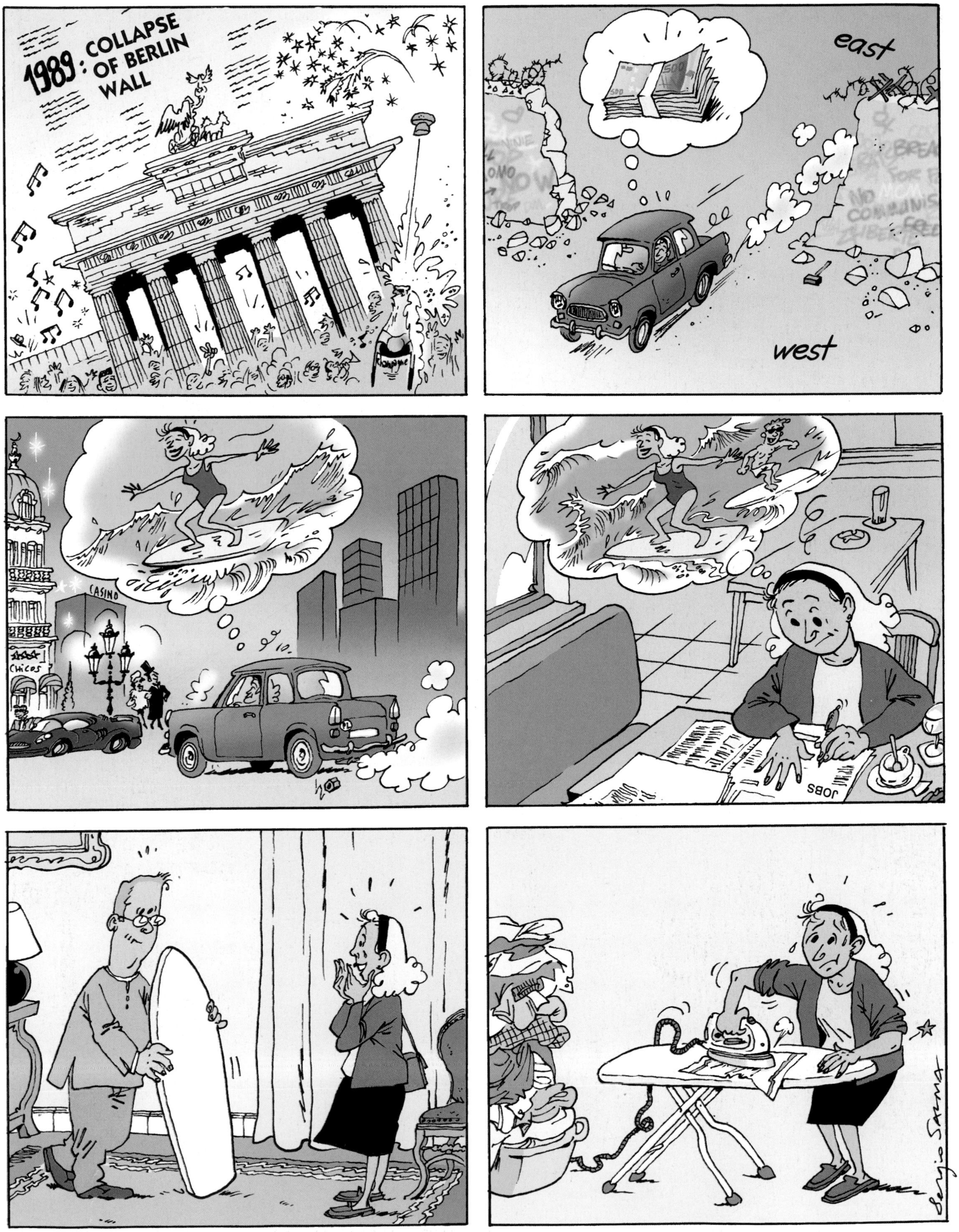
1989 : COLLAPSE OF BERLIN WALL
east
west
CASINO
CHICOS
JOBS

THE LEAST YOU CAN DO

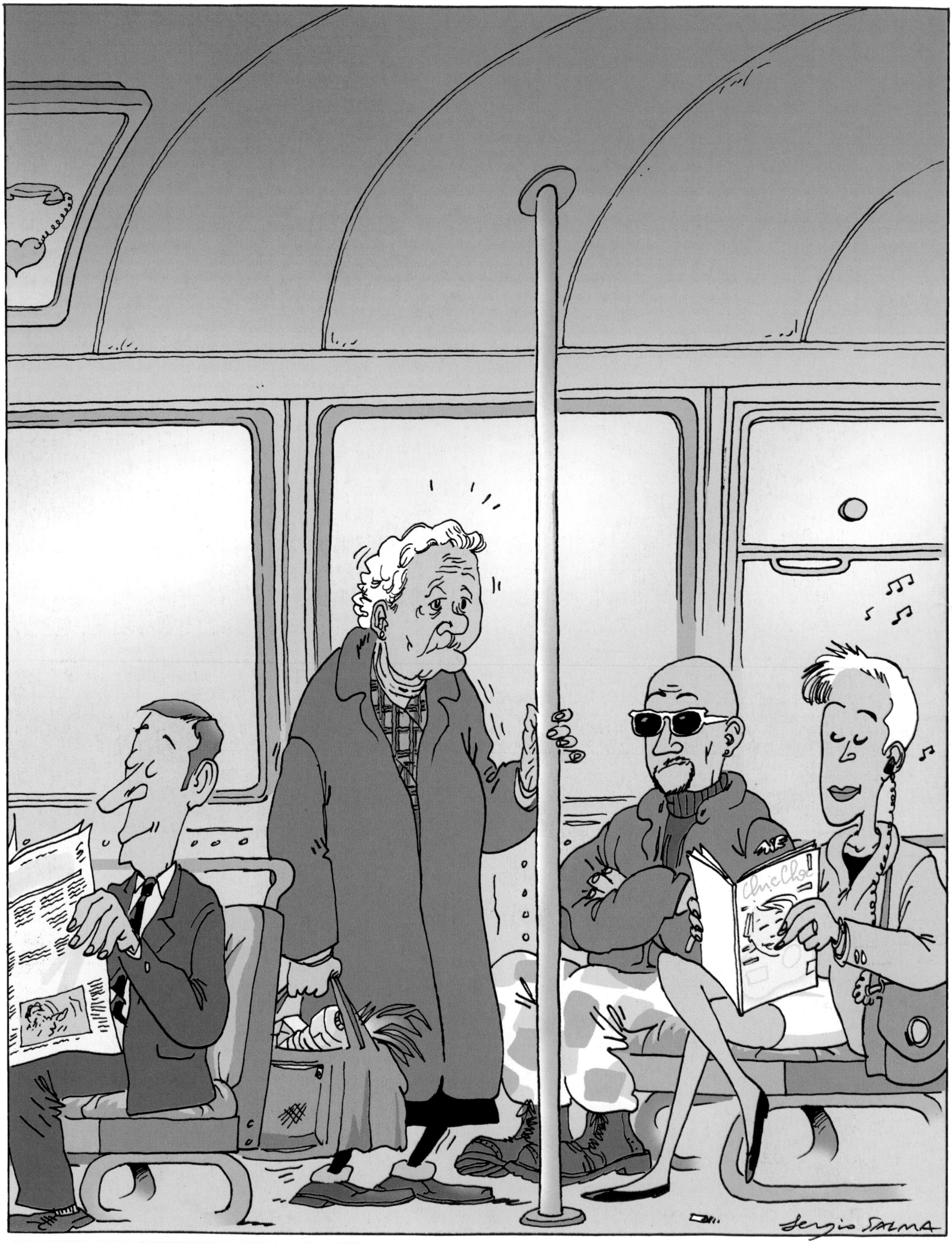
Chic Choc
Sergio SALMA

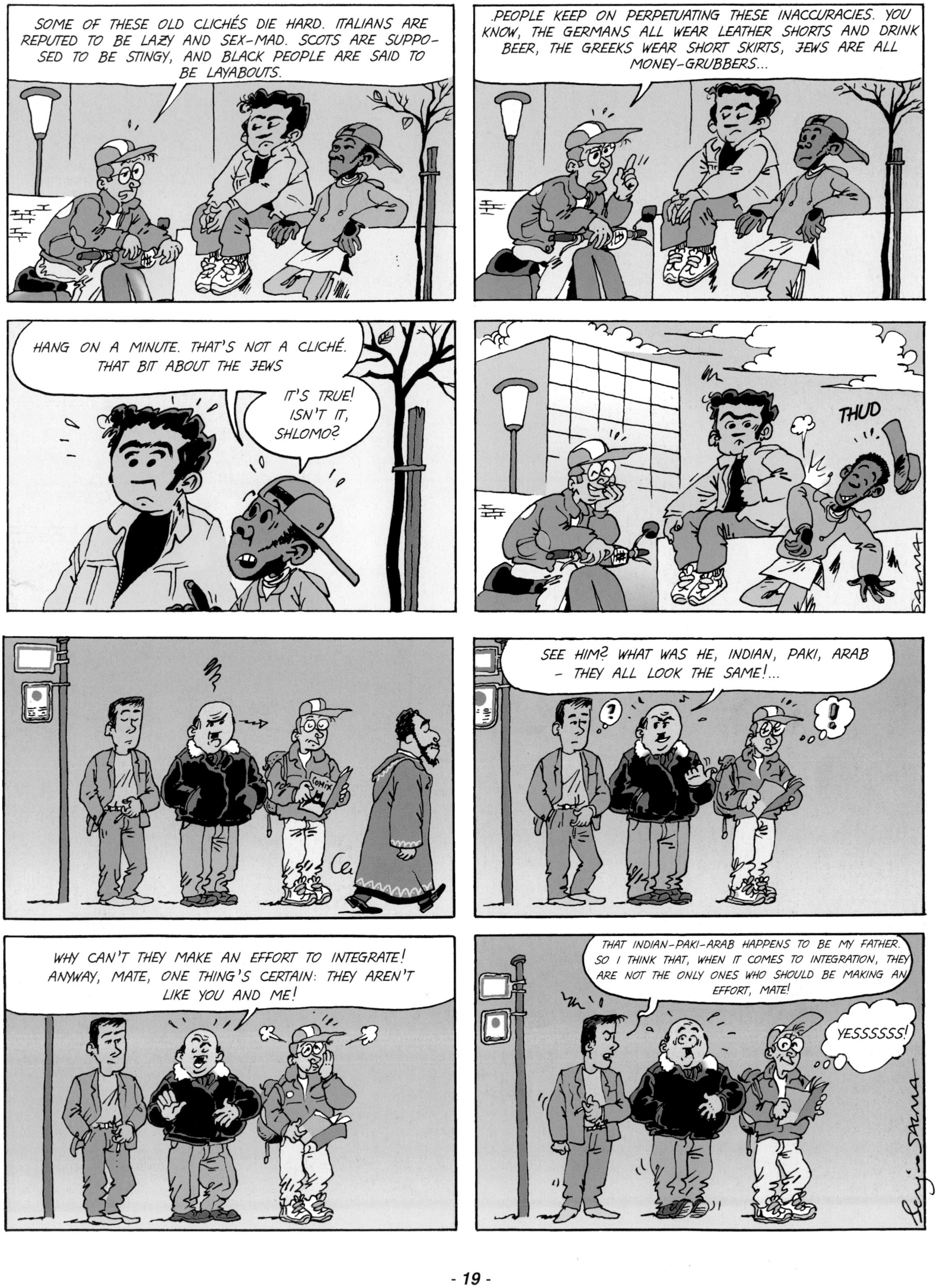
SOME OF THESE OLD CLICHÉS DIE HARD. ITALIANS ARE REPUTED TO BE LAZY AND SEX-MAD. SCOTS ARE SUPPOSED TO BE STINGY, AND BLACK PEOPLE ARE SAID TO BE LAYABOUTS.
.PEOPLE KEEP ON PERPETUATING THESE INACCURACIES. YOU KNOW, THE GERMANS ALL WEAR LEATHER SHORTS AND DRINK BEER, THE GREEKS WEAR SHORT SKIRTS, JEWS ARE ALL MONEY-GRUBBERS...
HANG ON A MINUTE. THAT'S NOT A CLICHÉ. THAT BIT ABOUT THE JEWS
IT'S TRUE! ISN'T IT, SHLOMO?
THUD
COMIX
SEE HIM? WHAT WAS HE, INDIAN, PAKI, ARAB - THEY ALL LOOK THE SAME!...
?
!
WHY CAN'T THEY MAKE AN EFFORT TO INTEGRATE! ANYWAY, MATE, ONE THING'S CERTAIN: THEY AREN'T LIKE YOU AND ME!
THAT INDIAN-PAKI-ARAB HAPPENS TO BE MY FATHER. SO I THINK THAT, WHEN IT COMES TO INTEGRATION, THEY ARE NOT THE ONLY ONES WHO SHOULD BE MAKING AN EFFORT, MATE!
YESSSSSS!

FINE FEATHERS MAKE FINE BIRDS?

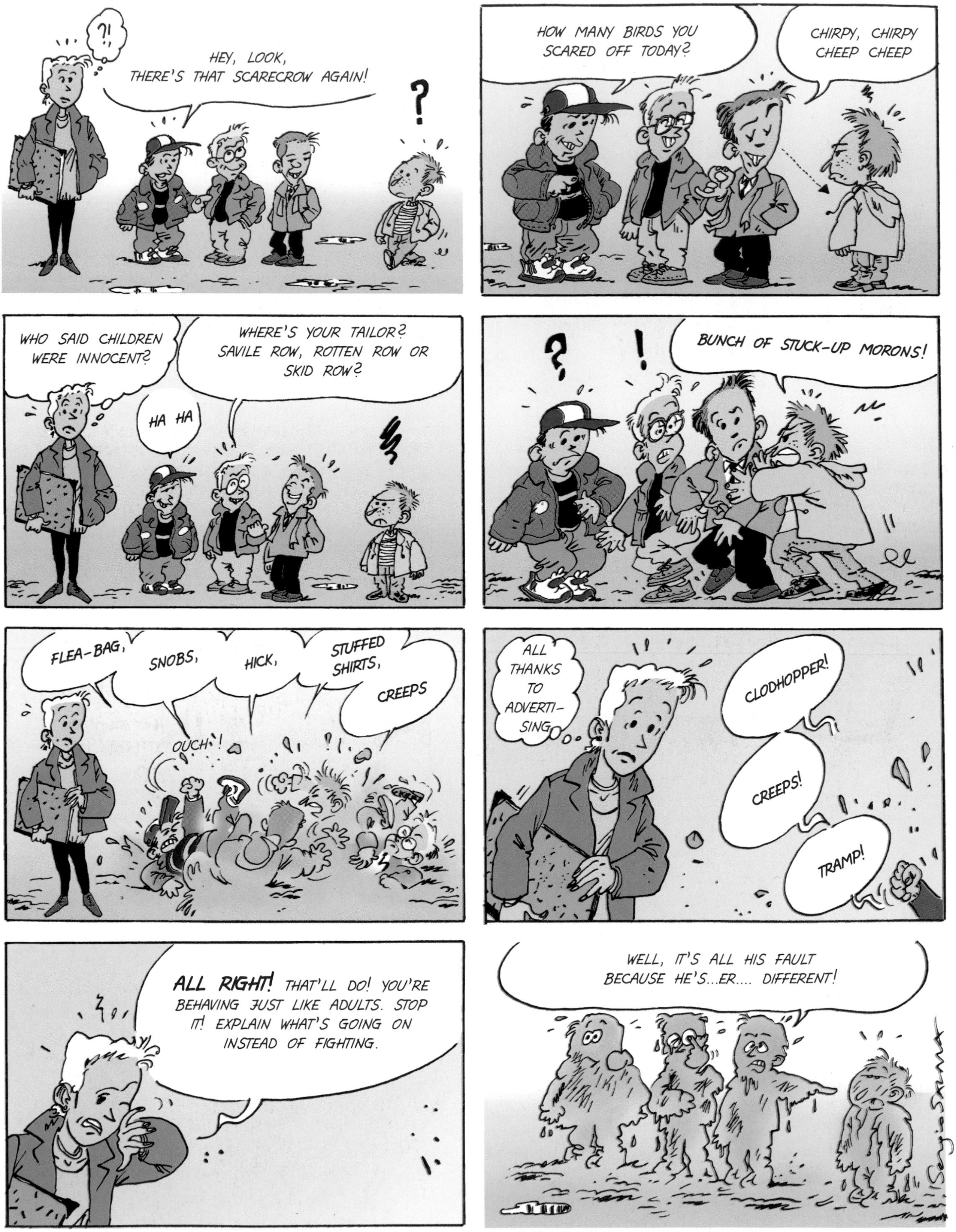
?!
HEY, LOOK, THERE'S THAT SCARECROW AGAIN!
?
HOW MANY BIRDS YOU SCARED OFF TODAY?
CHIRPY, CHIRPY CHEEP CHEEP
WHO SAID CHILDREN WERE INNOCENT?
WHERE'S YOUR TAILOR? SAVILE ROW, ROTTEN ROW OR SKID ROW?
HA HA
?
!
BUNCH OF STUCK-UP MORONS!
FLEA-BAG,
SNOBS,
HICK,
STUFFED SHIRTS,
CREEPS
OUCH!
ALL THANKS TO ADVERTI-SING
CLODHOPPER!
CREEPS!
TRAMP!
ALL RIGHT! THAT'LL DO! YOU'RE BEHAVING JUST LIKE ADULTS. STOP IT! EXPLAIN WHAT'S GOING ON INSTEAD OF FIGHTING.
WELL, IT'S ALL HIS FAULT BECAUSE HE'S...ER.... DIFFERENT!

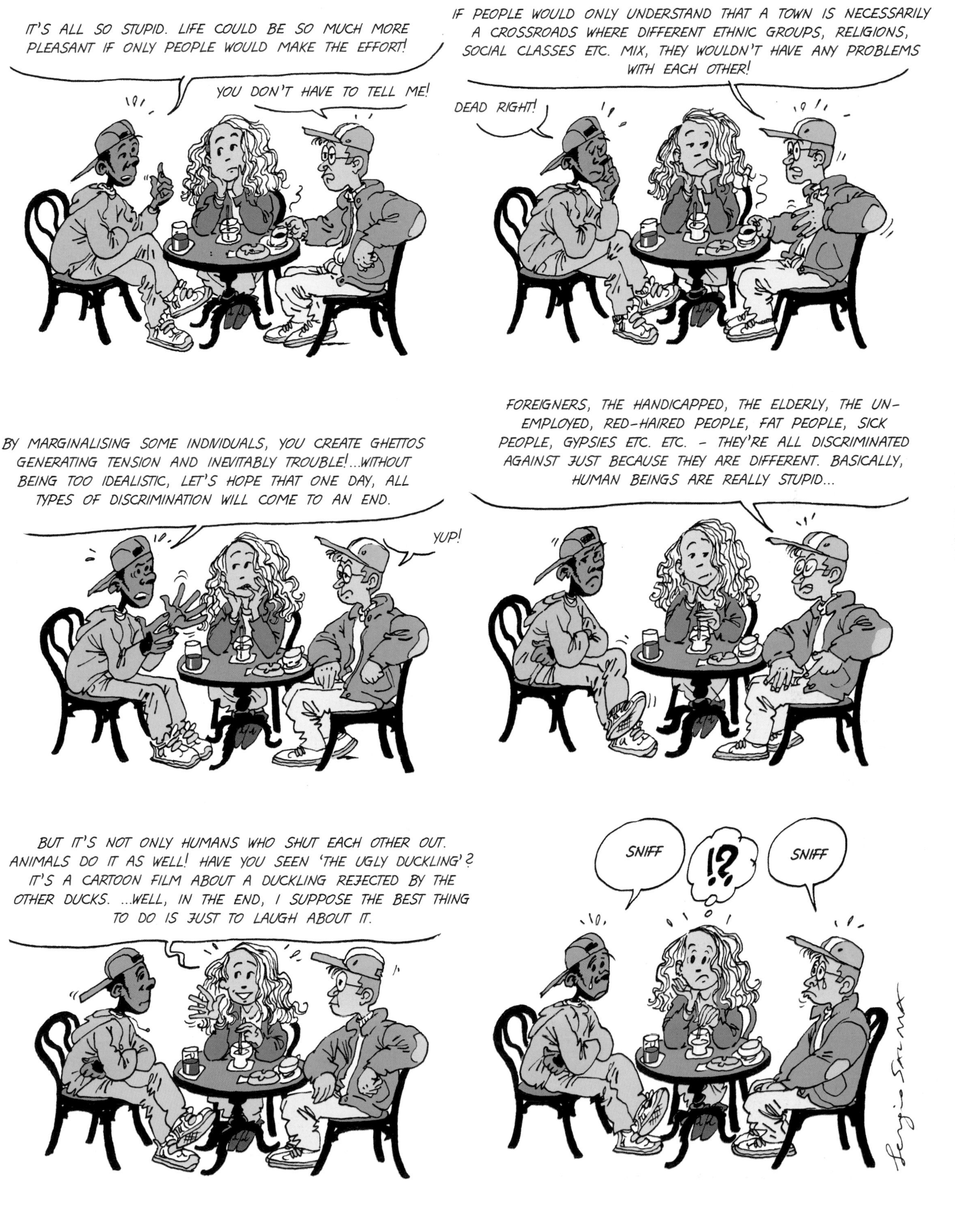
IT'S ALL SO STUPID. LIFE COULD BE SO MUCH MORE PLEASANT IF ONLY PEOPLE WOULD MAKE THE EFFORT!
YOU DON'T HAVE TO TELL ME!
IF PEOPLE WOULD ONLY UNDERSTAND THAT A TOWN IS NECESSARILY A CROSSROADS WHERE DIFFERENT ETHNIC GROUPS, RELIGIONS, SOCIAL CLASSES ETC. MIX, THEY WOULDN'T HAVE ANY PROBLEMS WITH EACH OTHER!
DEAD RIGHT!
BY MARGINALISING SOME INDIVIDUALS, YOU CREATE GHETTOS GENERATING TENSION AND INEVITABLY TROUBLE!...WITHOUT BEING TOO IDEALISTIC, LET'S HOPE THAT ONE DAY, ALL TYPES OF DISCRIMINATION WILL COME TO AN END.
YUP!
FOREIGNERS, THE HANDICAPPED, THE ELDERLY, THE UN-EMPLOYED, RED-HAIRED PEOPLE, FAT PEOPLE, SICK PEOPLE, GYPSIES ETC. ETC. - THEY'RE ALL DISCRIMINATED AGAINST JUST BECAUSE THEY ARE DIFFERENT. BASICALLY, HUMAN BEINGS ARE REALLY STUPID...
BUT IT'S NOT ONLY HUMANS WHO SHUT EACH OTHER OUT. ANIMALS DO IT AS WELL! HAVE YOU SEEN 'THE UGLY DUCKLING'? IT'S A CARTOON FILM ABOUT A DUCKLING REJECTED BY THE OTHER DUCKS. ...WELL, IN THE END, I SUPPOSE THE BEST THING TO DO IS JUST TO LAUGH ABOUT IT.
SNIFF
!?
SNIFF

THE FUTURE OF THE WORLD

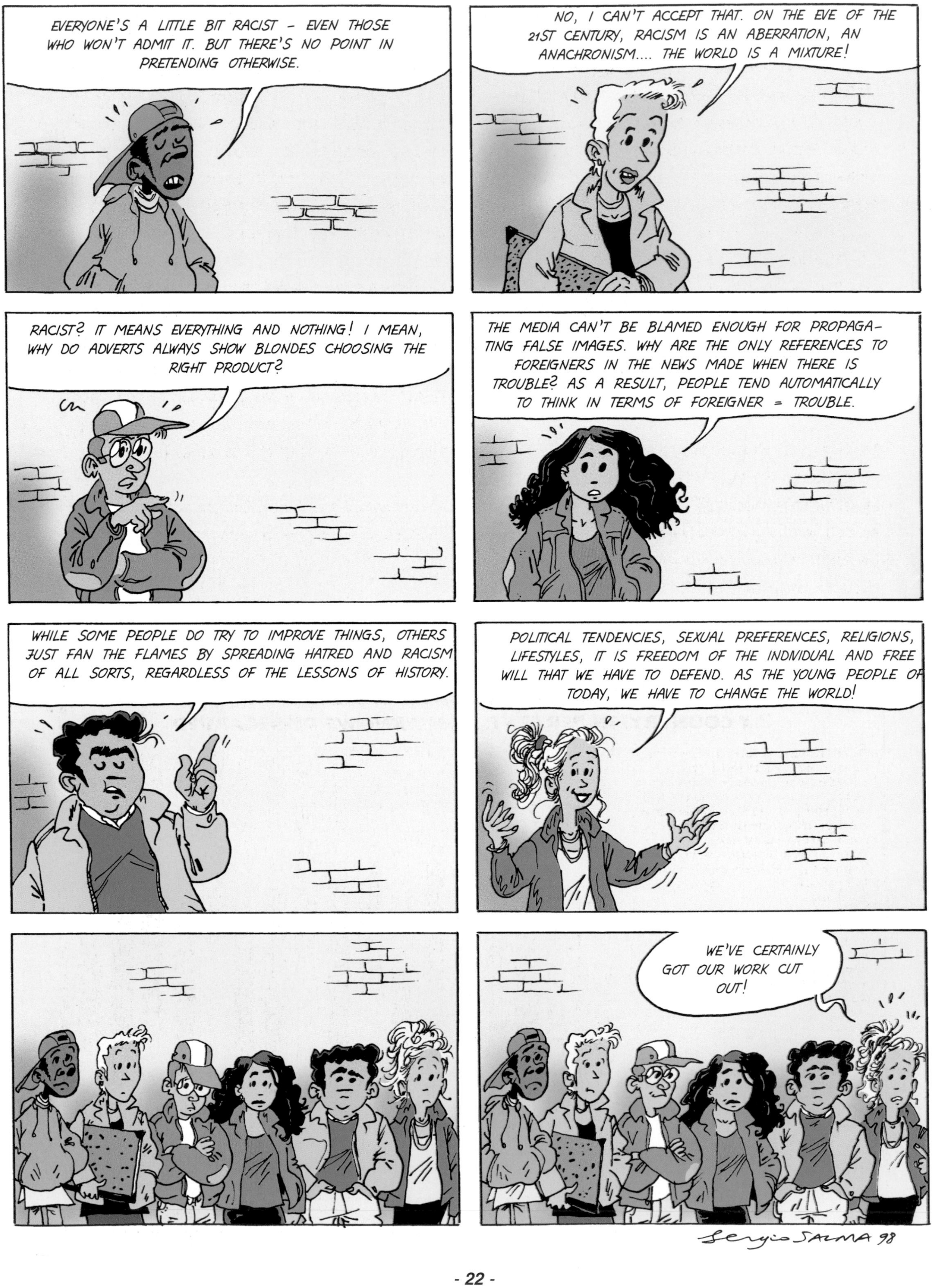
EVERYONE'S A LITTLE BIT RACIST - EVEN THOSE WHO WON'T ADMIT IT. BUT THERE'S NO POINT IN PRETENDING OTHERWISE.
NO, I CAN'T ACCEPT THAT. ON THE EVE OF THE 21ST CENTURY, RACISM IS AN ABERRATION, AN ANACHRONISM.... THE WORLD IS A MIXTURE!
RACIST? IT MEANS EVERYTHING AND NOTHING! I MEAN, WHY DO ADVERTS ALWAYS SHOW BLONDES CHOOSING THE RIGHT PRODUCT?
THE MEDIA CAN'T BE BLAMED ENOUGH FOR PROPAGATING FALSE IMAGES. WHY ARE THE ONLY REFERENCES TO FOREIGNERS IN THE NEWS MADE WHEN THERE IS TROUBLE? AS A RESULT, PEOPLE TEND AUTOMATICALLY TO THINK IN TERMS OF FOREIGNER = TROUBLE.
WHILE SOME PEOPLE DO TRY TO IMPROVE THINGS, OTHERS JUST FAN THE FLAMES BY SPREADING HATRED AND RACISM OF ALL SORTS, REGARDLESS OF THE LESSONS OF HISTORY.
POLITICAL TENDENCIES, SEXUAL PREFERENCES, RELIGIONS, LIFESTYLES, IT IS FREEDOM OF THE INDIVIDUAL AND FREE WILL THAT WE HAVE TO DEFEND. AS THE YOUNG PEOPLE OF TODAY, WE HAVE TO CHANGE THE WORLD!
WE'VE CERTAINLY GOT OUR WORK CUT OUT!
Sergio SALMA 98

COMBATING RACISM

A survey conducted across the European Union in the spring of 1997 shows racism and xenophobia to be reaching disturbing levels of intensity in the Member States: around 33% of those interviewed stated openly that they were 'fairly racist' or 'very racist'.

Those who say they are racist are more dissatisfied than others with their personal situation. They are afraid of unemployment, fear for the future and have no faith in their country's institutions and politicians. More of them also agree with the negative stereotypes applied to immigrants and minorities.

Many people who say they are racists are actually xenophobes: the 'minorities' who are the object of racist feelings in each country vary according to the colonial and migratory history of the country concerned and the numbers of refugees who have arrived in recent times. The results of the survey demonstrate the complexity of the racist phenom-

enon. Racist feelings coexist alongside a strong belief in the democratic system and respect for fundamental rights and freedoms. Most of those interviewed consider that society should be all-embracing and accord equal rights to all its members, including immigrants and those belonging to minority groups.

Opinion is more divided as to whether all members of minorities should enjoy these rights in all circumstances. Many believe that the rights of those considered to belong to 'problem groups', (i.e. illegal immigrants in the European Union, those who have committed criminal offences and those who are unemployed) should be restricted.

Those interviewed consider that the European institutions should play a greater part in combating racism.

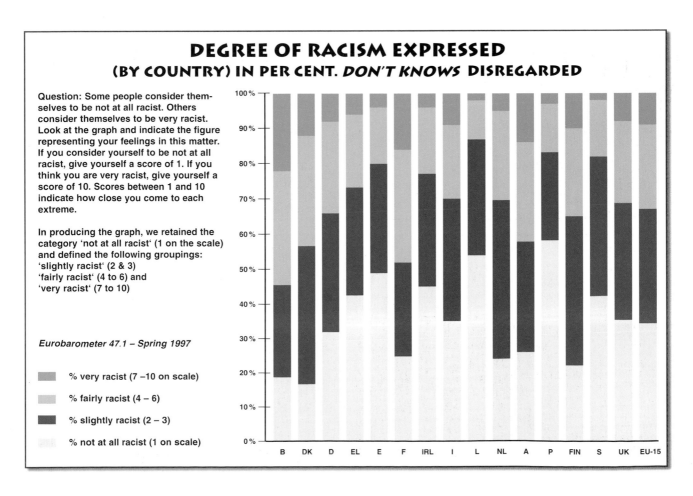

DEGREE OF RACISM EXPRESSED
(BY COUNTRY) IN PER CENT. *DON'T KNOWS* DISREGARDED

Question: Some people consider themselves to be not at all racist. Others consider themselves to be very racist. Look at the graph and indicate the figure representing your feelings in this matter. If you consider yourself to be not at all racist, give yourself a score of 1. If you think you are very racist, give yourself a score of 10. Scores between 1 and 10 indicate how close you come to each extreme.

In producing the graph, we retained the category 'not at all racist' (1 on the scale) and defined the following groupings:
'slightly racist' (2 & 3)
'fairly racist' (4 to 6) and
'very racist' (7 to 10)

Eurobarometer 47.1 – Spring 1997

- % very racist (7 –10 on scale)
- % fairly racist (4 – 6)
- % slightly racist (2 – 3)
- % not at all racist (1 on the scale)

B DK D EL E F IRL I L NL A P FIN S UK EU-15

ACTION TAKEN BY THE EUROPEAN UNION

1977

Joint Declaration on Fundamental Rights is signed by the European Parliament, the Council and the Commission

1986

The European Parliament adopts the first report of its Committee of Inquiry into the rise of fascism and racism in Europe.

The Council, European Parliament and Commission adopt a joint declaration against racism and xenophobia.

1989

The Community Charter of the Fundamental Social Rights of Workers mentions the importance of combating every form of discrimination, including discrimination on the grounds of sex, colour, race, opinion and beliefs.

1990

The European Council adopts a resolution at the Dublin Summit on the struggle against racism and xenophobia.

The European Parliament adopts the second report of its Committee of Inquiry calling for increased action at European level.

1991

The European Council adopts a resolution at the Maastricht Summit promising to act 'clearly and unambiguously' to counter the growth of racism and xenophobia.

1992

The Economic and Social Committee adopts a resolution on racism, xenophobia and religious intolerance.

At the Edinburgh Summit, the European Council adopts a third resolution against racism calling for 'vigorous and effective measures to be taken throughout Europe to control this phenomenon both through education and legislation'.

1993

Several European Parliament resolutions are adopted on racism and xenophobia and the danger of right-wing extremist violence.

The European Council adopts a fourth declaration at the Copenhagen Summit condemning racism and xenophobia. It states that it has 'decided to intensify the efforts to identify and root out the causes' of racism and pledges 'to do the utmost to protect immigrants, refugees and others against expressions and manifestations of racism and intolerance'.

1994

At the Corfu Summit, acting on a Franco-German initiative, the European Council decides to set up a Consultative Committee on racism and xenophobia to make practical recommendations favouring 'tolerance and understanding'. It agrees to develop a global strategy at Union level to combat racism. Also in 1994, at the Essen Summit, the European Council asks the Commission 'to step up its discussions' in particular in the areas of education and training, information, the media, police and the judiciary.

In its White Paper on Social Policy, the European Commission announces its intention to 'press for specific powers to combat racial discrimination to be included in the Treaty'.

A European Commission Communication on immigration and asylum policies devotes the last chapter to combating racial discrimination and to tackling racism and xenophobia.

A European Parliament resolution on racism and xenophobia calls for an EU directive to reinforce existing provisions in the Member States' legislation.

1995

The Consultative Committee presents its final report, containing wide-ranging recommendations for action to the European Council meeting in Cannes. The European Council asks the Consultative Commission to extend its work, in cooperation with the Council of Europe, to study the feasibility of setting up a European monitoring centre on racism and xenophobia.

Two European Parliament resolutions on racism, xenophobia and anti-Semitism press for safeguards to equal employment opportunities, irrespective of age, race, sex, disability or beliefs.

The Social Affairs Council and the Education Council adopt resolutions on combating racism in work and in educational systems.

The European Commission proposes a Council Decision to designate 1997 as the European Year Against Racism. The Commission indicates the specific role it could play in complementing national action. The key areas identified are: promoting integration and opening pathways to inclusion, promoting equal opportunities and reducing discrimination; raising public awareness and combating prejudice; preventing racist behaviour and violence; monitoring and punishing racist crime; international cooperation; strengthening anti-racist legal provisions including at European level.

The Social Dialogue Summit of employer and trade union representatives adopts a joint declaration on the prevention of racial discrimination and xenophobia and the promotion of equal treatment at the workplace.

1996

The European Parliament, Economic and Social Committee and Committee of the Regions give backing to the 1997 European Year Against Racism proposal.

The Consultative Committee completes the feasibility study. The European Council asks this Committee to continue its work until the Moni-toring Centre is established and gives the goahead to the European Year.

1997

Member States and the European Parliament agree to set up a monitoring centre in Vienna. It will have a dual role: to take stock of and evaluate racist and xenophobic phenomena and analyse their causes and to formulate concrete and practical proposals to combat them.

The Heads of State or Government incorporate protection of human rights and basic freedoms into the new Treaty on European Union concluded at the Amsterdam Summit.

1998

The European Commission presents an overall action plan for combating racism.

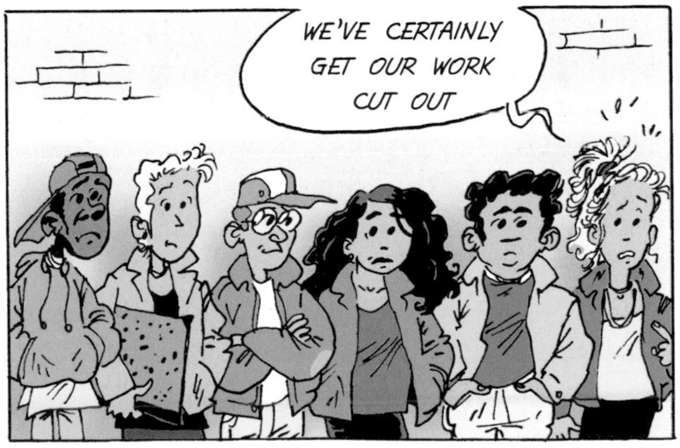
WE'VE CERTAINLY GET OUR WORK CUT OUT

THE TREATY OF AMSTERDAM AND THE INTERNATIONAL CONVENTIONS

The Treaty of Amsterdam Chapter 1

General principles underlying the Union

The Union is founded on the principles of liberty, democracy, respect for human rights and fundamental freedoms and the rule of law, principles which are common to the Member States.

The Union shall respect fundamental rights, as guaranteed by the European Convention for the Protection of Human Rights and Fundamental Freedoms signed in Rome on 4 November 1950 and as they result from the constitutional traditions common to the Member States, as general principles of Community law.

The Union shall respect the national identities of its Member States.

'The Union shall provide itself with the means necessary to attain its objectives and carry through its policies.'

Non-discrimination Article 6a

'Without prejudice to the other provisions of this Treaty and within the limits of the powers conferred by it upon the Community, the Council, acting unanimously on a proposal from the Commission and after consulting the European Parliament, may take appropriate action to combat discrimination based on sex, racial or ethnic origin, religion or belief, disability, age or sexual orientation.'

European Convention for the Protection of Human Rights and Fundamental Freedoms, 1950 Article 14

'The enjoyment of the rights and freedoms set forth in this Convention shall be secured without discrimination on any ground such as sex, race, colour, language, religion, political or other opinion, national or social origin, association with a national minority, property, birth or other status.'

United Nations International Convention on the Elimination of All Forms of Racial Discrimination, 1965 Article 1

In this Convention, the term 'racial discrimination' shall mean any distinction, exclusion, restriction or preference based on race, colour, descent, or national or ethnic origin which has the purpose or effect of nullifying or impairing the recognition, enjoyment or exercise, on an equal footing, of human rights and fundamental freedoms in the political, economic, social, cultural or any other field of public life.

WHY SHOULD WE TAKE ACTION AT EUROPEAN LEVEL?

European identity
The struggle against racism is an inseparable part of the European identity. The need to build the foundations for a wider and deeper sense of community between peoples who had too often opposed each other in violent conflict was an integral part of the ideals that inspired the founders of the Community.

Democracy
The European Union must be built on a society which values difference, by representing the needs and reflecting the interests and values of all its citizens, irrespective of their ethnic, religious, national or cultural identity. This is essential for democratic development and the legitimacy of existing governments and their institutions.

No Member State is spared this problem and no social or cultural group can be certain never to become the victim[1].

Respect for human rights
The respect for human rights and basic freedoms set out in the Treaty, and the right to equal treatment and freedom from discrimination are core principles underlying all Community policies.

[1] Communication from the Commission on racism, xenophobia and anti-Semitism, COM (95) 653 final.

Economic and social rights and development

Racism and xenophobia constitute a serious threat, not only to the stability of European society, but also to the smooth functioning of the economy[1].

European economies are not using their diverse workforce to its full potential[1].

Discrimination interferes with the free movement of people and services by preventing those who suffer from discrimination from obtaining jobs, housing or the services they seek[2].

Variations in national levels of protection against racism will discourage people likely to suffer from racism from moving within the European Union to Member States where protection is insufficient[2].

Full social, economic and political participation by all citizens is integral to European development. But racism both excludes and, at the same time, feeds on exclusion. When people feel threatened or pushed aside in a divided society, they will want to push others aside.

The fight against racism and xenophobia is closely linked to the general employment situation and to migration and integration policies such as access to education and accommodation[1].

---

[1] *Joint declaration by the social partners on the prevention of racial discrimination and xenophobia and promotion of equal treatment at the workplace.*

[2] *1997 European Year Against Racism, opening conference report.*

EUROPE AGAINST RACISM

Whereas racism, xenophobia and anti-Semitism are opposed to fundamental rights, as referred to in Community law, recognised in international declarations/instruments and endorsed in constitutional traditions,

Whereas there is a continuing presence of racism, xenophobia and anti-Semitism throughout Europe, which poses a major challenge for our societies and which calls for the mobilisation of all partners in counteracting these phenomena,

Whereas the Council and the Member States have recognised this challenge in designating 1997 as the European Year Against Racism,

We, the undersigned, affirm:

– the fundamental right of everyone to live free of discrimination or harassment on the basis of race, colour, religion or national or ethnic origin;

– the necessity to build partnerships in order to join forces in the struggle against racism, xenophobia and anti-Semitism.

We, the undersigned, commit ourselves:

– to strengthen our action to fight racism, xenophobia and anti-Semitism in all areas of life, thereby making use of all resources and instruments available;

– to cooperate to this end with all relevant partners;

– to initiate, stimulate and promote the dissemination of good practice and experience;

– to further relevant measures, including European and national codes of conduct.

We, the undersigned, intend:

– to actively take part in the European Year Against Racism;

– to actively take part in the process of European mobilisation launched through the European Year Against Racism.

We call upon all European institutions, public authorities, private organisations and individuals at both European, national and local level, to contribute in everyday life, at school, at the workplace and in the media, to the struggle against racism, xenophobia and anti-Semitism.

Wim Kok
Prime Minister of the Netherlands
President in office of the Council

José María Gil-Robles Gil-Delgado
President of the European Parliament

Jacques Santer
President of the European Commission

BUILDING BRIDGES BETWEEN CULTURES

One of the greatest challenges for European societies today is how they will develop to embrace the increasing mix of cultural groups. Policies have evolved using concepts, values and models considered to be the norm under the dominant culture of society. The result is an emphasis on similarities and homogeneity reinforcing a feeling of exclusion of those who do not fit into this definition.

Culture is defined here in its widest sense, that is going beyond ethnic or national definitions to include factors such as gender, education, social background and religion.

Culture can be defined following Hofstede[(1)] as 'the collective programming of the mind which distinguishes the members of one group or society from those of another.'

This programming starts at birth and continues right into adulthood. It takes place in the family, at school and at work. The common values, beliefs and attitudes which make up a group's culture are learned at an early age and work at a conscious and unconscious level. They are shaped through power structures, institutions and social practices. It is these processes which differentiate a group and render it specific. They give an individual an identity, a sense of belonging and a point of reference.

People who are similar by virtue of belonging to the same group trust each other more easily. The greater the difference, the greater the distrust and the harder it is to find common ground. This applies in both private and professional life.

Combating racism requires self-examination. Racism today has moved on from blatant and overt action to more subtle and hidden manifestations based on the non-acceptance of difference. It involves a hidden system of exclusion dividing those who are and those who are not perceived to be part of a group.

(1) Hofstede, G., *Culture's consequences*, Sage Publications, London, 1980.

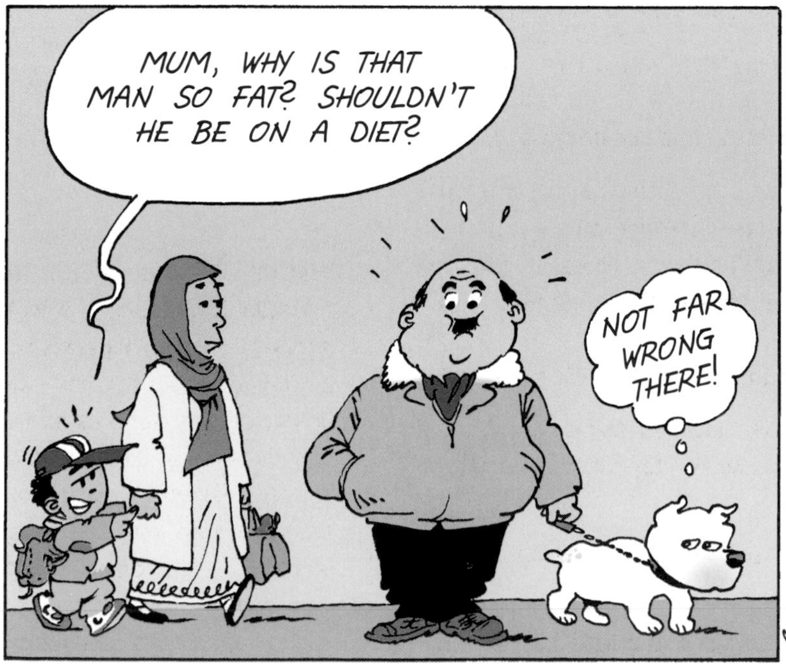
MUM, WHY IS THAT MAN SO FAT? SHOULDN'T HE BE ON A DIET?
NOT FAR WRONG THERE!
Sergio Salma

STEPS IN INTERCULTURAL COMMUNICATION

● **STEP 1**

a state of ignoring differences, represented by attitudes such as 'our way is best'.

● **STEP 2**

a state of awareness of differences gained through intercultural contact, communication and observation – 'other people have different ways of doing things from us'.

● **STEP 3**

a state of tolerance, respecting 'they are different from us' but without attaching a value judgement.

● **STEP 4**

a state of accepting, valuing and using differences positively – 'let's work together in a mutually beneficial manner'.

A LOOK AT DEFINITIONS AND CONCEPTS

'**Europe** is a multi-cultural and multi-national society and is enriched by this diversity. But the continuing presence of racism within our societies cannot be ignored. Racism affects everyone. It eats away our communities, creating insecurity and fear.'

Pádraig Flynn, European Commissioner

'**Creativity** can only take place where there is a difference.'

Yehudi Menuhin, violinist and human rights defender

'**Racism**... begins by being the promotion of a difference, real or imaginary, to always justifying an aggression. An aggression which is founded upon a failure to understand the other, the inability to accept difference and to engage in dialogue.'

Mario Soares, former President of Portugal

'**Prejudice**: unfavourable, negative feelings about somebody or a group of people, formed without knowledge, reason or fact.

Power: the ability to put things into action, to have authority and control.

Difference between racism and prejudice: while pre-judice can mean dismissing people even before you know anything about them, you may not have the power to influence their lives negatively. Racism, however, is bound up with the way a whole society works and involves having the power to put coloured prejudices into action. The majority of a society have the power over the minority and can intentionally or unintentionally exercise racism. Thus, racism involves having the power to discriminate against and disadvantage people because they are different.'

British Youth Council

'**Racism** is the belief that some people are superior because they belong to a particular race. Racists define a race as a group of people with common ancestry. They distinguish different races from one another by physical characteristics, such as skin colour and hair texture. In fact, there are no clear differences, and especially no significant differences that matter. Recent research shows that race is an imagined entity. 'Race' has no biological basis. The word 'racism' is also used to describe abusive or aggressive behaviour towards members of an 'inferior race'. Racism takes different forms in different countries, according to history, culture and other social factors. A relatively new form of racism sometimes called "ethnic or cultural differentiation" says that all races or cultures are equal but they should not mix together to keep their originality. There is no scientific proof of the existence of different races. Biology has only determined one race: the human race.'

'**Intolerance** is a lack of respect for practices or beliefs of others. This is shown when someone is not willing to let other people act in a different way or hold different opinions. Intolerance can mean that people are not treated fairly because of their religious beliefs, their sexuality, or even their clothes and hairstyle. Intolerance does not accept difference. It lies at the basis of racism, anti-Semitism, xenophobia and discrimination in general. It can often lead to violence.'

'**Equality** is the state of being equal. It means that no person counts more than another, whatever his or her parents are, whatever his or her social position is. Of course, people are not identical to one another in their interests, abilities, and lifestyles. So equality for people is about having the same rights and the same chances. People must have equal opportunities to succeed in education or work, depending on their own efforts. Equality will only be a reality when people have the same access to housing, social security, civil rights and citizenship.'

Interculturalism 'is the belief that we become richer persons by knowing and experiencing other cultures, that we add to our personality because of encounters with other cultures. Different people should be able to live together, although they have different cultural backgrounds. Interculturalism is about accepting and respecting differences. People that believe in interculturalism believe they can learn and profit from meeting other cultures.'

UNITED for intercultural action

'There are a number of different steps down the path to active discrimination, violence and even ethnic cleansing and genocide.

CATEGORISATION... making generalisations and putting our experiences into categories makes it easier to deal with the world around us. We distinguish and divide people and groups into pigeonholes ...

STEREOTYPING... when we pigeonhole people, it's tempting to use stereotypes... Stereotypes are judgements based on insufficient facts. Both positive and negative stereotypes exist... but if we create a negative stereotype and then exaggerate it, it becomes dangerous and it can lead to...

PREJUDICE... is formed by ideas based on a cocktail of emotion and insufficient facts. A prejudice is often formed without any basis of truth and yet is accepted unquestioningly. Often there is a contrast between us and them. Prejudices can lead to hostile behaviour towards the group in question. So out of a prejudice can come the following reactions:

AVOIDANCE... avoiding the group, not talking to them, not wanting to meet them

VERBAL ABUSE... speaking negatively of the group and to the group

DISCRIMINATION... whereas prejudice is an attitude, discrimination is the behaviour of holding the group in low estimation, treating them badly, rewarding them less than others, boycotting and excluding them

VIOLENT ABUSE... by taunting, pestering, threatening, harassing or damaging the group's personal belongings

ELIMINATION... by isolating, banning, killing, lynching, genocide and ethnic cleansing'

CSV Media (UK), Towards Equality, *a manual for youth groups working on anti-discriminatory media initiatives*

'Immigration is a constant thread running through the fabric of human history, creating and enriching cultures rather than threatening them.'

Russell King, University of Sussex, 1991

'We are at an important crossroads now, facing perhaps one of the bitterest battles we have ever fought. Fundamentalist beliefs of all sort are taking hold around the world... Racism is a human invention, a relatively modern one and I don't think it is inevitable.'

Professor Patricia Williams, 49th Reith Lecturer, 1997

BIBLIOGRAPHY

A compendium published by the European Commission contains the complete text of most of these measures. Entitled *The European Institutions in the fight against racism: Selected texts*, it can be obtained free of charge from the European Commission Representations in each Member State or from the European Commission, Directorate-General V : Employment, Industrial Relations and Social Affairs – Documentation.
Fax: (32-2) 296 23 93
Catalogue number: CE-01-96-438-EN-C
ISBN number: 92-827-9841-0.

Declaration by the Council and the representatives of the Governments of the Member States, meeting within the Council of 16 December 1997 on respecting diversity and combating racism and xenophobia
Official Journal C 1, 3.1.1998

Declaration by the Council and the representatives of the Governments of the Member States, meeting within the Council of 24 November 1997 on the fight against racism, xenophobia and anti-Semitism in the youth field
Official Journal No C 368, 5.12.1997

Developing an intercultural outlook
Office for Official Publications of the European Communities
ISBN number: 92-828-1338-X

Racism and xenophobia in Europe
Eurobarometer 47.1, Spring 1997, Directorate-General V

European compendium of good practice for the prevention of racism at the workplace
Office for Official Publications of the European Communities
ISBN number: 92-828-1960-4

An action plan against racism
COM (1998) 183 final of 25 March 1998

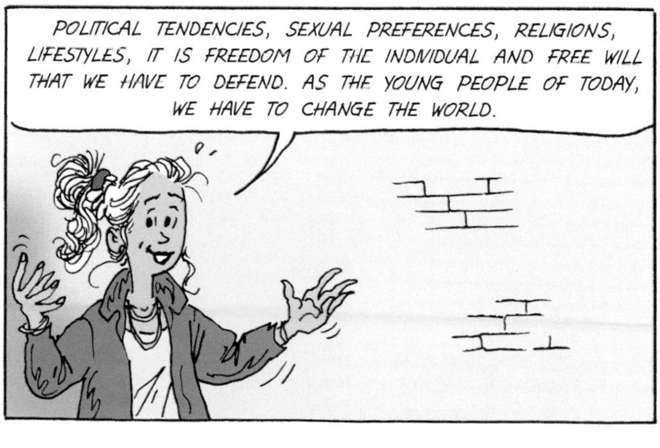

POLITICAL TENDENCIES, SEXUAL PREFERENCES, RELIGIONS, LIFESTYLES, IT IS FREEDOM OF THE INDIVIDUAL AND FREE WILL THAT WE HAVE TO DEFEND. AS THE YOUNG PEOPLE OF TODAY, WE HAVE TO CHANGE THE WORLD.

European Commission

What? Me? A racist?

Luxembourg: Office for Official Publications of the European Communities

1998 — 31 pp. — 21 x 29.7 cm

ISBN 92-828-4019-0

The European Union is determined to combat discrimination on grounds of sex, race, ethnic origin, religion or belief, disability, age or sexual orientation. This humorously written and informative pamphlet has been designed for teachers to use when addressing the subject of racism with young people.